Initiation and Conversion

INITIATION AND CONVERSION

Major Presentations Given at the 1984 National Meeting
of the Federation of Diocesan Liturgical Commissions

Regis A. Duffy, O.F.M.
James D. Shaughnessy
Barbara O'Dea, D.W.
James Lopresti, S.J.
Editor: Lawrence J. Johnson

THE LITURGICAL PRESS
Collegeville, Minnesota

Cover design by Mary Jo Pauly

THE LITURGICAL PRESS
Collegeville, Minnesota 56321

Library of Congress Catalog Card Number: 85-080746

Contents

Copy
well done

Foreword

In 1976 the members of the Federation of Diocesan Liturgical Commissions (FDLC) gathered in Indianapolis to reflect on the Rite of Christian Initiation of Adults (RCIA), especially from the perspective of the ongoing renewal of the local parish as the faith community within which the RCIA takes place. At a time when the rite was practically unknown to the majority of American Catholics, the meeting's participants were provided with knowledge, motivation, and inspiration to encourage diocesan parishes to undertake a new approach to adult initiation.

Eight years later, at the National Meeting of Diocesan Liturgical Commissions, the FDLC returned to the RCIA as the theme of its reflection. What was only a vision at Indianapolis had become an experienced reality in an ever increasing number of communities. This experience has indeed enriched and strengthened the fabric of parish life. It has summoned forth a reshaping of the Church's self-image and posture. It has deepened insights, broadened understandings, and even surfaced new and often disturbing questions regarding our very lives as Christians. Thus the experience of the past years motivated the Federation to probe anew the meaning and potentialities of the RCIA. This occurred at the 1984 Sacramento meeting with its theme of "Initiation/Conversion." This volume contains the four major addresses given at that gathering.

Conversion, both individual and communal, touches the very core of the RCIA and indeed of the whole Christian life. It is this multi-dimensional reality which is explored by Fr. Regis Duffy in "The Praxis of Conversion." The praxis of conversion embraces "the decisions and actions that betray the real meanings and values of our experience." The model of Christian conversion is the catechumenate. But does the reality mirror or distort this model? Father Duffy, with biblical discernment and careful precision, reflects on five crucial questions that impact upon our theory and practice of conversion in community. (1) "To what extent does the cross still decisively redefine the praxis of conversion?" (2) "To what extent does the Word of God continue to introduce complexity into the ongoing conversion of both catechumens and baptized?" (3) "To what extent does the lack of ecclesial change and mission call into question the prevailing notions and praxis of conversion?" (4) "How would our narrations of conversion be expanded and changed by the answers we give to questions one through three?" (5) "Is liturgy an accurate measure of and challenge to conversion in the community?" If our praxis of conversion fails to match our theory then we have not, says Father Duffy, as yet captured "the spirit of conversion that the catechumenal process symbolizes."

Conversion presumes neither inertia nor isolation. It is the personal dynamics of the conversion process that Sr. Barbara O'Dea first explores in "The Process of Conversion." She compares this process to a story that has five parts: relative paradise, crisis, descent into hell, turning point, and homecoming. The journey of conversion begins with a period of relative stability, passes through change and choice, and finally ends with surrender and deep integration. The Church offers persons undergoing such a journey several dimensions which uphold the process and dynamics of conversion. First, there is a tradition wherein "seekers can discover their own stories." There is also community, i.e., a shared awareness of identity and a consciousness of mission. Finally, there is ritual whereby "participants are brought into touch with the archetypal experience which is the source of this common identity and purpose." Sister concludes by sketching five basic implications of a conversion-oriented theology: (1) "focus on conversion requires a restoration of a kingdom-vision"; (2) "conversion must be understood as the starting point and the condition of Christian discipleship"; (3) "human experience must become the starting point for pastoral ministries"; (4) "Catholics must be called to corporate ecclesial conversion"; (5) "Catholics must come to recognize baptism as a vocation."

A Church which is just beginning to live again as a conversion-oriented community must confront a vast panorama of pastoral issues. In "Conversion and the Rite of Christian Initiation of Adults," Fr. James Shaughnessy touches on several of these. He warns against isolating the RCIA from the other working elements in the Christian community. He calls attention to the overall implications of the RCIA in regard to other sacramental expressions of the Church's life, e.g., the anomaly of having two different patterns for initiation, one for adults and another for children. He reminds us that baptism is not a "once and for all" reality but rather an ongoing event which must constantly permeate the life of the community. Drawing on his pastoral experience, Father Shaughnessy exhorts us to study the complete RCIA document, to avoid anything that smacks of the "herd" approach, to provide catechetical instruction based on God's Word, to give more thought on how to sustain the newly initiated, and to reflect on how to differentiate between the baptized and the non-baptized seekers.

Fr. James Lopresti gave the meeting's concluding address entitled "Visions and Challenges." In probing various dimensions of a Church moving on to the future, he utilizes two principles enunciated by Vatican II. The first is the metaphor of the Church being a "pilgrim people of God." It is a people in motion, a people who possess a participant's knowledge of the gospel, a people characterized by a pluralism resulting from opposites in dialogue, a people marked by that contemplation and discernment which result from surrendering to the Word. The second principle used by Father Lopresti is that of *actuosa participatio*. Active participation, he reminds us, is not merely a matter of folk or dance groups, but "first of all a claim about the spirit which animates a community, a spirit given in power to a people as a people, immersed in the death-resurrection of Christ." The catechumenal experience is refocusing the image of the Church as it moves from an ordination model to a baptismal model. It is this revitalized model which expresses and highlights our fundamental human solidarity. Active participation, concludes Father Lopresti, means "recognizing the one bread and the one body by worshipping as an assembly finding as much real presence in one another as in the Word and the bread and the cup." It means "recognizing in the broken bread the surprising crucified one."

The Federation of Diocesan Liturgical Commissions is grateful to The Liturgical Press for publishing these addresses.

Lawrence J. Johnson

Executive Secretary
Federation of Diocesan Liturgical Commissions

The Praxis of Conversion

1

The Praxis of Conversion

REGIS A. DUFFY, O.F.M.

Choreographers have a difficult task. They must not only create gestures and motions in response to a musical score but, often enough, must be able to symbolize an experience, feeling or a story. In 1928 the famous Russian impresario Diaghilev commissioned Sergei Prokofiev to set the parable of the Prodigal Son to music. The result was a masterful musical symbolization of conversion in all its complexity. But imagine if you were then asked to do the choreography of this conversion.

The early dances in the ballet, which portray the relationships of the son to his father and brother and the subsequent escape to a life of irresponsibility and freedom, are graphic and telling. But the creative genius of Prokofieff and his choreographer were challenged in trying to shape the music and motion of conversion as the young man returns to his father. Anyone who has seen M. Barishnikov recreate the role of the prodigal son will remember this scene. The dance consists in the tentative and painful hobbling home of the son. Motion and music accurately conspire to remind us how complex any turning in human life is.

The first example of this complexity is how conversion is generally understood and experienced in both theology and the human sciences. In reviewing the extensive literature from these disciplines, [1] it is readily apparent that privatized notions of religion are transformed into privatized conceptions and experiences of conversion. As we shall see, the blame for this one-sided notion of conversion rests as much with parishes that are not yet communities as with individuals who believe that they can welcome God but not the "others." This situation is not significantly changed by a theoretical discussion of the ecclesial dimension of conversion. Nor can it be assumed that the sum total of "private" conversions equals a converted Church.

A second example of this complexity is the multidimensional nature of conversion. From a sociological viewpoint Lofland and Skonovd, for example, distinguish six conversion motifs: intellectual, mystical, experimental, affectional, revivalist, and coercive. [2] These investigators arrived at this schema by examining accounts of conversion for qualitatively different ways in which people evaluate and react to these experiences. In assessing the conversion accounts of Augustine, for example, we might expect to find several of these motifs in play accompanied by various emphases at different points of the experience. This schema of conversion motifs serves as a reminder of the complexity of our subject. [3]

A third example of the complex nature of conversion is the kinds of interdisciplinary discussion usually engendered. When psychology or sociology analyzes the nature of conversion from their particular viewpoint, they also provide valuable insights into some dimensions of the experience that might otherwise be neglected in a theological discussion. On the other hand, if theological theory and praxis are correctly focused on all the dimensions of conversion, the human sciences can also benefit from an interdisciplinary dialogue. Ultimately, however, there is a limitation to such exchanges. Christian conversion is, in the last analysis, measured by its goal, the Kingdom of God. This goal suggests a more demanding notion and praxis of community, commitment, and purpose than any human science.

This introduces a final element in our introductory remarks on the complexity of conversion—the question of "praxis." This word as used in this essay means the decisions and actions that betray the real meanings and values of our experience. Just as the Christian believes that the Kingdom of God is already an inchoate experience begun among us, so Christian conversion is perceived as a question of God's initiative and our response. Conversion is a question of praxis, that is, our current response to God's meaning for both our lives and the destiny of his creation. While sociological definitions of conversion may include the ideas of a radical change of identity, meaning, and "root reality,"[4] the Christian experience of God's action in our midst radically enlarges such definitions to include a transformed future, a "new creation," the Kingdom of God.

The classical model of Christian conversion that incorporates all of these dimensions is, of course, the catechumenate. With the restoration of this process, the Church has a praxis model of conversion that can serve as a criterion for the continuing transformation of the Christian community and its members, both initiated and candidates, on every level of contemporary living. When the implications of this model are taken seriously, then we can be sure that the complexity of conversion will be respected. Some of these catechumenal implications for the theory and praxis of conversion will be indicated later in this essay.

From this brief overview it should be apparent that the complex dimensions of conversion suggest many issues that still demand attention from both the theologian and the pastoral minister. What are some of the structural consequences, for example, of our religious practice and how do these touch on our participation in ongoing conversion?[5] Is turning from social sin an integral and practical part of conversion? What is the connection between individual conversion and ecclesial renewal? When a Christian community has the vaguest of eschatologies, does this affect conversion in its midst? Is there a connection between life-stages and the commitment that conversion entails? When there are self-serving notions and praxis of conversion in the Christian community, how is liturgy a help or a hindrance toward greater honesty? What are some of the crucial connections between conversion and mission?

Within the limits of this essay, I cannot hope to examine all these questions. The methodology of this paper is shaped by questions about the praxis of the local Christian community. No matter what theories of conversion are taught or preached, a contrary praxis can make it difficult to welcome God's initiating and gracious invitation to walk with others toward the Kingdom. With this in mind, I would suggest five questions that attend to the praxis of conversion in the community. First, to what extent does the cross still decisively redefine the praxis of conversion? Second, to what extent does the Word of God continue to introduce complexity into the ongoing conversion of both catechumens and baptized? Third, to what extent does the lack of ecclesial change and mission call into question the prevailing notions and praxis of conversion? Fourth, how would our narrations of conversion be expanded and changed by the answers we give to questions 1 through 3? Finally, is liturgy an accurate measure of and challenge to conversion in the community?

The Cross and Conversion

To what extent does the cross still decisively redefine the praxis of conversion? There is a rich and illuminating literature about the meaning of conversion in the Old Testament.[6] With God's unexpected solution of the cross, however, all definitions and experience of conversion are radically transformed. And yet, the praxis of the Christian communities and individuals would sometimes lead us to believe that there need be no shadow of the cross in our lives. This is usually not an explicit repudiation of the cross but rather a quiet reduction of its meaning to ritual signs, artistic symbols, and Good Friday readings. To return to our catechumenal model, Christian communities and their members walk in the way of conversion to the extent that the challenging meaning of the cross compels them to reassess the most basic meanings, values, and goals of their lives.

Both theologian and pastoral minister can easily find practical examples of this principle in the New Testament. In the gospel accounts, the disciples' reluctance to accept Jesus' approaching death (e.g., Matt 16:21-23) as central to his meaning and mission is not a literary device.[7] It is easily forgotten that discipleship presupposes a continuing conversion. The very reluctance of the disciples to accept the events of Good Friday as anything but a disaster is a telling reminder of how profound a conversion we must continue to undergo throughout our lives. The post-Easter events (e.g., Luke 24:13-21) graphically demonstrate that the meaning of the cross casts both Easter and the nature of our conversion and discipleship in a startling new light. To learn to accept the cross is to be able to welcome the good news of Easter.

Paul perceives this same problem in the would-be disciples at Corinth. Some of these Christians have developed a very selective and self-serving notion and praxis of conversion that does not include the appropriation of the cross as a crucial element. Paul's ringing reminder of his teaching still challenges the Church today: "I determined that while I was with you I would speak of nothing but Jesus Christ and him crucified" (1 Cor 2:2).

Paul's reexamination of the meaning of the cross is, in effect, a delineation of the nature of conversion. The very words that he employs to describe contemporary reaction to the cross also imply how radically unexpected the nature of conversion is: *skandalon* (Greek for "stone of stumbling") and *moriā* ("absurdity/foolishness"). In other words, the cross as the ultimate symbol of God's justifying and gratuitous redemption can paradoxically become an obstacle to those whose expectations are deceived by the self-gift of Jesus.

Conversion in the new covenant is defined by the saving self-gift of Jesus on the cross. Resurrection is God's unconditional validation of the centrality of that action: "the Jesus who was handed over to death for our sins and raised up for our justification" (Rom 4:25). God's plan for new life shines out in the obedience of this second Adam: a single righteous act brought all acquittal and life (Rom 5:18). [8] The obedience of the crucified Lord is both the model and continuing test of conversion.

We should exercise a Pauline caution here. The obedience of those in conversion is not to be confused with a "law and order" attitude and response. We do not earn the gift of salvation because of our good conduct: "If justice is available through the law, then Christ died to no purpose"(Gal 2:21). Rather it is the obedience of Christ which enables us to be obedient and thus, in the way of conversion. The result of this kind of obedience is an openness to the complexity of living in a committed gospel fashion at different stages of life, each with its own challenges. Paul states this obedience of conversion in practical terms: "While we live we are constantly being delivered to death for Jesus' sake . . . ." (2 Cor 4:11). [9]

The purpose of this brief scriptural review of the theology of the cross and its relation to conversion was to aid us in responding to the question about the praxis of contemporary conversion. [10] From the vantage point of the cross, conversion loses its customary profile. Just as the cross is a challenge to our false security and a reminder of our need for redemption, so conversion is a gradual appropriation of Christ's commitment to the proclamation and building of the Kingdom of God. Conversion in the new covenant is fleshed out by the meaning of the cross. We acquire the outlook, attitudes, and values of Christ (Phil 2:5).

This converted like-mindedness with Christ manifests itself in the new meanings that we give our lives. First, conversion under the cross means a life on account of others: "He died for all so that those who live might live no longer for themselves . . . ." (2 Cor 5:15). If sin is a selfish alienation from God's meanings and values, then conversion entails an imitation of the self-gift of Jesus who in living and dying enfleshed the Kingdom's meanings and values. If this is true, then the question of how we call others to such conversion under the cross suggests a reevaluation. How do we teach the meaning of the cross?

Self-gift, rooted in a continuing conversion tied to the meaning of the cross, presupposes some awareness of the nature of our charisms and gifts at each life-stage as well as a review of some of the current internal and external obstacles that would prevent our service to others. The disastrous results of not taking these tasks of self-awareness seriously are visible in the naive pietism of some spiritualities and in the deepening frustration of serious Christians who seek formation in the mission of the Church. Just as Christ's self-awareness continued to shape his mission to others, even to the death on a cross, so Christians in conversion must realistically frame their commitment to the meaning of the cross within a renewed appreciation of the contexts and challenges of their time. An elderly person, for example, who wishes to appropriate the new tasks of conversion in the last stages of his or her life must reassess the internal danger of despair and the external danger of a culture that does not regard the self-gift of older people as significant or valuable.

The second practical test of life-mindedness with Christ is an ongoing dialogue between the local church and its individual members about the ways in which participation in the death of Christ is to be lived out so that the Christian community may indeed be a place of shared values. This type of dialogue entails much more than the statement of the Christian community's position on a specific moral issue. This ecclesial process invites a shared responsibility for fleshing out the ramifications of Christ's self-gift within a specific cultural and social situation. The Young Catholic Workers' movement earlier in this century or, more recently, "base communities" in South America and the "RENEW" programs in this country are examples of inviting all who call themselves Christian to become active participants in owning the attitudes of a crucified Lord and thus, responding to the Pauline challenge: "Conduct yourselves, then, in a way worthy of the gospel of Christ" (Phil 1:27).

A Rousing Word

Our second question about the praxis of conversion asks to what extent does the Word of God continue to introduce complexity into the ongoing conversion of both catechumens and baptized? The biblical understanding of the Word of God as his dynamic presence calling us to conversion is a familiar theoretical statement which may be contradicted for many people by their experience of poorly celebrated liturgies of the Word, irrelevant homilies, and the apparent ineffectiveness of that Word to change significantly the distorted world that they inhabit. To reassess the problem correctly, another question must be asked: to what extent does the Word from the cross (1 Cor 1:18) transform the Word of God?

A graphic response to that question can be found in the conversion process of early Christians. Although it seems that the resurrection was announced as the decisive event in the earliest preaching of the gospel, it quickly became apparent that the meaning of Jesus' death also had to be more closely examined and appropriated. [11] Thus, in praxis, the proclamation of the Word of God as a call to conversion was profoundly affected by the meaning given to the related events of the cross and resurrection. [12]

But Luke provides us with a paradigm for conversion as the Word of God disclosing the meaning of the cross and resurrection in his perceptive narration of the disciples' walk to Emmaus (Luke 24:13-35). Although these two followers are called disciples, it is readily apparent that God's ways are not yet their ways. They know the facts of Jesus' suffering and death but can find no meaning here to appropriate. In Luke's carefully crafted story, Jesus walks with these confused people as the living Word who discloses the meaning of Good Friday so that Easter Sunday can be believed. The Master unfolds the Word of God "beginning with the prophets" as a preparation for under-standing the formative meaning of the cross, and therefore, the mission of Christ—one who endured suffering so as to enter his glory (Luke 24:26).

Luke has, in effect, sketched what is the process of discipleship—an acceptance of the implications of conver-sion as seen in the cross and resurrection. [13] Jesus does not inform as much as form and enable these novice disciples to accept the power of the cross as validated in his risen person, and so to "walk" with him in the biblical sense of conversion. Luke's description of the reaction of these disciples ("hearts burning within them," Luke 24:32) is not poetical. Rather it is an accurate biblical test for those who walk toward the Kingdom, supported by the surprising power of God's salvation in Christ. [14]

In brief, the living Word of God is, as I have argued elsewhere, [15] a praxis-event that both discloses our real rela-tion to the cross and enables us to accept its meaning for our lives. Paul's summary of the Word that transforms us is still accurate: "Our preaching of the gospel proved not a mere matter of words for you but one of power; it was carried on in the Holy Spirit and out of complete convic-tion" (1 Thess 1:5). [16] In moving through each life-stage, then, Christians perceive the new implications of their con-version through the power of that revealing Word.

Neither conversion, therefore, nor its complementary dimension of discipleship are static experiences. Matthew gives us a working model for this problem of the imperfect disciple whose conversion must continue in the story of Jesus walking on the water (Matt 14:22-33). Peter's response to this apparition is a request to walk toward Jesus. At the Master's invitation, Peter begins his walk on the stormy sea but becomes frightened and cries out, "Lord, save me!" As Jesus rescues him, he remarks, "How little faith you have! Why did you falter [*edistasas*]?" (Matt 14:31).

As I. P. Ellis has pointed out, it is not Peter's faith but rather his lack of total conviction that is in question. The verb that Matthew employs *(edistasas)* highlights this situation, since it indicates "the person concerned is divided in his conviction . . . the facts are present but action on them is lacking."[17] Peter's continuing education as disciple demands further evaluations and decisions. The apostle's ongoing conversion is shaped by his continuing to accept Christ's power and to move past the commitments already taken.[18]

The Christians who hear the Word of God will find themselves crying out, as Peter, "Lord, save me!" The ensuing need to make further decisions and better commitments inevitably reforms the way that we hope for the Kingdom of God. Conversion, after all, is a prelude to participation in God's victory over distorted meanings and his gathering of a divided creation. There is no continuing conversion worthy of the name that does not link a Christian's future hope in the Kingdom with the very decisions and actions that help build that future now.

There is a pedagogical corollary to this discussion of how the Word of God introduces complexity into the process of our conversion. The local Christian community has a responsibility to enable its members to participation in the task of hearing anew and proclaiming the gospel message. The effectiveness of the liturgy of the Word and the relevancy of preaching still leave much to be desired. On the other hand, diocesan-wide programs, such as "RENEW," provide the opportunity for sharing the Word of God in small groups. The sacramental celebration of the Word of God in reconciliation, at weddings, and at funerals can have a particular effectiveness because of the specific problems and challenges that these occasions provide. In other words, conversion is not a process in some Christians' lives because the Word of God has yet to be taken seriously.

Turning in Circles?

Theologies of conversion are made irrelevant fairly often by the praxis of conversion in specific situations and communities. A crucial context for conversion is the Christian community. Without such a context theories about conversion will be inadequate if not irrelevant. This concern prompts our third question: to what extent does the lack of ecclesial change and mission call into question the prevailing notions and praxis of conversion? In other words, when the community lacks a sense of direction, how does this affect the continuing conversion of its members?

In sociological or psychological discussion of conversion, we expect that the definition and role of "the group" will play a definite and circumscribed role. [19] Some recent theological analyses of conversion have also concentrated on the relation of J. Fowler's stages of faith to conversion. [20] While the comparison has some interest, Fowler's stages do not have a strong ecclesial component and thus, both conversion and faith tend to have a more restricted meaning. What is surprising is that not a few theologies of conversion seem to have no real role for the Christian community in the process. The RCIA, of course, states this ecclesial dimension of conversion very clearly—"in the midst of the community of the faithful" (par. 4). It further indicates that the very nature of initiation as conversion involves both candidates and baptized in mutual and continuing process of renewing these commitments.

In effect, the RCIA presents a theory that is based on the praxis of conversion in the early Church and that is designed to encourage renewed praxis within the contemporary Church. But the process is always implemented within a specific community that has, for better or worse, an operational definition of its purpose and mission. The point of our question is, then, to inquire about a typical parish where administrative and financial concerns as well as the responsibilities of sacramental and educational ministries can absorb the attention and efforts of the parish team. In such a parish there may be functional ideas of ecclesial renewal and mission (e.g., an annual parish retreat or special efforts to help the poor at Thanksgiving) that do not include the more profound call to question the social and cultural structures that perpetuate radical sin in acceptable forms. Do such situations affect the very process of conversion?

Within the New Testament perspective, the connections between the formation of a community that proclaims conversion through the gospel and a commitment to mission are obvious. It is the very nature of new covenant conversion to proclaim and share the liberating power of the risen Lord as mediated by the Spirit. Even after we make allowance for the imminent eschatology of the earliest New Testament writings, the overriding conviction that sharing in the work of the gospel is formative of a community "turned toward the Lord" remains. [21].

The implications and demands of long-range conversion are expanded considerably when reseen within the context of the Christian community's mission. God's call invites individuals with all their gifts to enter a community whose task is to announce Jesus' message about the Kingdom—the goal of conversion. But personal sin within and without the community is not the only obstacle to that proclamation. There are the many levels of social sin whose structures systematically mute the good news of the gospel.

One of the subtle dangers to continuing conversion and mission even within the Christian community is that we may collude with these radically sinful structures in naive and unconscious ways. As G. Baum reminds us, "what is proper to social sin is that it is not produced by deliberation and free choice . . . . According to the biblical description, social sin is committed out of blindness. People are involved in destructive action without being aware of it."[22]

To return to our current question, how important is the specific Christian community's awareness of their continuing communal need for conversion and their praxis of mission? From the above discussion, the answer should be obvious: conversion becomes quickly privatized, or at least isolated from its roots when operating in an ecclesial vacuum.[23] On the other hand, there is a reciprocal strengthening of gospel purpose and conversion in a community which knows how to call out new commitments to mission from all its members and to seek renewed ecclesial awareness with the help of these very same members.[24]

Unedited Narrations

In recent years there has been a growing awareness that the classical narrations of conversion, as found, for example, in Augustine's *Confessions,* are an important element in clarifying and furthering that process in the future chapters of our lives.[25] My purpose here is not to review this large body of literature[26] but to focus on the corollaries of what we have already discussed in this article. The fourth praxis question might be stated in this way: how would our narrations of conversion be expanded and changed by our discussions of the cross, the Word of God, and ecclesial mission?

An excellent pedagogy in the narrations of conversion is offered in the Johannine readings employed for the third, fourth, and fifth Sundays of Lent—the catechumenal Sundays of the scrutinies. In the carefully crafted stories of the Samaritan woman (John 4:4-42), the man born blind (John 9:1-41), and the raising of Lazarus (John 11:1-44), we are witnesses to the impact that Jesus must have if anyone is to turn continually to God. A favorite Johannine theme in these stories is the revelatory and "seeing" character of conversion and faith. [27] In each story, questions are raised that cannot be avoided: "Where do you expect to get this flowing water? . . . . Could this not be the Messiah?" (John 4:11, 29); "Who is he, sir, that I may believe in him?" (John 9:36); "Why could he not have done something to stop this man from dying?" (John 11:37). The answer in each situation lies in the recognition of Jesus as Savior. Those who are in the path of conversion ask clarifying questions that help them recognize the saving and justifying action of the Lord in their experience.

The cross as a test of conversion probes our narrations with this question: is your experience characterized by the obedience of self-gift or that of the "law"? Much investigation of conversion in both the human sciences and theology centers on the ethical components of our experience. In other words, in what ways has conversion forced us to change our conduct? But conversion, seen through the prism of the cross, does not allow us to focus exclusively on our private need for salvation or a purely ethical response to sin but rather, urges us to face the redemptive need of our world. The obedience engendered by conversion is a response to that need, modeled on the imitation of Jesus' self-gift—the Son who learns obedience (Heb 5:8) and who recognizes our weakness (Heb 4:15). This perspective of obedience permits us to review our

stories with new insight for it heightens our awareness of
how God has gifted us for the service of others. In assessing the state of his own conversion, Paul outlines this continuing formation to the obedience of the cross: "We are
afflicted in every way possible, but we are not crushed;
full of doubts, we never despair. . . . Continually we carry
about in our bodies the dying of Jesus . . . ." (2 Cor 4:8,
10). N. Baumert in his extensive study of this Pauline
passage points to three stages in this growth as Christian:
the first steps of conversion expressed in faith and initiation; then the ensuing effort in each life-stage to be someone
on account of others; and the final actualization of the
meaning of Christ's death for us in our identification with
him. [28] When we look to our stories to see the meaning of
what God has done for us, we will always find the profile
of how we have been prepared to serve and thus, to be
like Christ (Heb 10:5-9).

The Word of God poses a second question for our stories
of conversion: does his Word still contextualize and redefine
the words of our narrations? Expressed differently, does
the living Word of God continue to provide new insight
about the meaning of our past experience so as to give us
a sense of direction and purpose for our future? Conversion is not a question of a unique and definitive decision
that need never be made again. The complexity of our own
stories give lie to such simplistic interpretations of God's
salvation at work in our world.

The process of conversion can be short-circuited by the
self-serving versions of our stories that excuse us from further decision and self-gift. God's Word, on the other hand,
heard in the midst of his Church, brings together the
strands of our inter-connected narrations so that we once
again perceive our mission with and for others. But this
hard won solidarity is the result of struggling with the im-

plications of the Word of God within the contexts of our stories. Rather than excuse us from deepened self-gift as we grow older, our stories, seen in the light of God's Word, invite us to the unexpected tasks of the final stages of our lives. The test of better listening to God's Word and our words is the questions that our stories prompt us to ask: "Where did I expect to find flowing water? . . . . Could this not be the Messiah?" etc.

A third way of questioning our experience emerges from the nature and mission of the Christian community that God has given us as both guide and companion on the path of conversion. There are those who believe that conversion is experienced and lived out despite that flawed community we call the Church. These Christians still have a lesson to learn from Paul. In a profound sense, Paul's letters are as much a personal testimony to his own journey of conversion within and on account of the disappointing Christian communities he served as they are a reminder about the theology of salvation and conversion. Therefore, our stories of conversion bear reexamination as we ask: who are the significant communities in our lives that have called us to walk with them?

A Restless Praise

Some years ago R. Haughton spoke eloquently of the relation between our ecclesial praise and our continuing conversion: "The prophetic calling comes to the Church in the cultic community and by it and . . . it is there that she learns the language that defines her and which she must use in carrying out her mission . . . ."[29] As correct as this is from the objective viewpoint, the praxis situation forces us to still ask: is liturgy an accurate measure of and challenge to conversion in the community? In pastoral terms, the question might be phrased in this way: do our well-filled churches on Sunday assure us that our meanings and God's are the same?

Honest worship and liturgy come not only from what God is doing among us but from the response that he enables us to give. A "knowing, active, and fruitful" liturgy (Constitution on the Sacred Liturgy, 1, par. 11) indicates the converted attitudes, values and meanings that permit us to praise the unearned graciousness of God's saving work among us. Worship and liturgy are symbolic actions that reveal and clarify meanings. With Christ, all praise of God was radically transformed: "But Jesus offered one sacrifice for sins and took his seat forever at the right hand of God . . . . By one offering he has forever perfected those who are being sanctified" (Heb 10:12, 14). The writer of the Book of Hebrews spells out the conversion corollaries of this fact: "let us draw near in utter sincerity and absolute confidence, our hearts sprinkled clean from the evil which lay on our conscience and our bodies washed in pure water" (Heb 10:22). R. Jewett, in commenting on these verses, captures their meaning with the phrase a "worshipful pilgrimage."[30] Honest liturgy accompanies and enlightens the journey that conversion continues to be.

Since conversion permits us to welcome God's view on the purpose and goal of his "new creation" that Christ inaugurated, our honest liturgy reflects this change in our own vision. Our narrations about God's part in our lives constantly fuel our prayer and span our personal experience and the shared experience of the Christian community as it prays. But this description of authentic liturgy as the new covenant dialogue of God and his people is premised on our participation as well as his. It is at this point that our question about liturgy as an accurate reflection of conversion in the community takes on a prophetic ring.

The Dance Continues

The choreographer of conversion is always God, but all of us are invited to dance in uninterrupted fashion until a peaceable Kingdom is fully realized. A major obstacle to this final eschatological purpose occurs when the Christian community allows conversion to become privatized in its midst. The telltale sign of this distorted conversion is usually a lack of mission within a Christian community. This situation indicates that the meaning of the cross of Christ and the Word of God are not being fully understood and appropriated by gathered Christians.

The RCIA in classical fashion summarizes the theory of how conversion and its symbolization in initiation always point toward the mission of a renewed Church to proclaim the Kingdom of God. But the praxis of the catechumenate does not necessarily match its theory. If the baptized see no challenge in the conversion of the catechumens, if the Christian community does not feel compelled to reexamine its operational values and priorities while it fosters a catechumenal program, if liturgy remains a cause of ennui or consolation but not an imperative to long together for the Kingdom of God, then we have yet to capture the spirit of conversion that the catechumenal process symbolizes. [31]

We are perhaps too easily consoled by theological theories when we do not wish to face our praxis. The prophetic warning to the Church at Ephesus may then be addressed to us: "I know your deeds, your labors, and your patient endurance. . . . I hold this against you, though: you have turned aside from your early love" (Rev 2:2, 4). But the dance goes on: prodigal sons and daughters still turn around and God still waits to put the ring on their finger and to clothe them with Kingdom garments of celebration. And we, we are the servants of this dance.

Notes

1. L. Rambo, "Current Research on Religious Conversion," *Religious Studies Research* 8 (1982) 146–59.

2. J. Lofland and N. Skonovd, "Conversion Motifs," *Journal for the Scientific Study of Religion* 20 (1981) 373–85.

3. For a further discussion, see R. Duggan, "Sociological Perspectives on Conversion," *Conversion and the Catechumenate*, R. Duggan, ed. (New York: Paulist, 1984) 120–44; T. Long and J. Hadden, "Religious Conversion and the Concept of Socialization: Integrating the Brainwashing and Drift Models," *Journal for the Scientific Study of Religion* 22 (1983) 1–14.

4. See Lofland and Skonovd, "Conversion Motifs," 375, for typical definitions.

5. For the background discussion of critical theology, see G. Baum, *Religion and Alienation. A Theological Reading of Sociology* (New York: Paulist, 1975) 193–223.

6. For an overview of the subject, see M. B. Dick, "Conversion in the Bible," R. Duggan, ed., *Conversion and the Catechumenate*, 43–63; here, 43–53.

7. See J. P. Meier. *The Vision of Matthew* (New York: Paulist, 1978) 115–18; for some of the background issues, see G. Friedrich, *Die Verkündigung des Todes Jesu im Neuen Testament* (Neukirchen-Vluyn: Neukirchener Verlag, 1982) 25–44.

8. See U. Schnelle, *Gerechtigkeit und Christusgegenwart. Vorpaulinische und paulinische Tauftheologie* (Göttingen: Vandenhoeck & Ruprecht, 1983) 74–75; also, E. Käsemann, *Commentary on Romans* (Grand Rapids: Eerdmans, 1980) 157.

9. The Greek verb for "being handed over" is used elsewhere in the New Testament to refer to the death of Jesus; see W. Popkes, *Christus Traditus: Eine Untersuchung zum Begriff der Dahingabe im Neuen Testament* (Zurich: Zwingli, 1967) 193–94.

10. I have examined more extensively some of the scriptural background for the meaning of the cross in *On Becoming a Catholic: The Challenge of Christian Initiation* (San Francisco: Harper & Row, 1984) esp. 1–36.

11. For an extended discussion of this process, see Friedrich, *Die Verkündigung* 14–24.

12. For one possible reconstruction of the steps of awareness about the meaning of Christ's death in the early Christian communities, see J. Roloff, "Anfänge der soteriologischen Deutung des Todes Jesu (Mark 10:45 and Luke 27:22)," *New Testament Studies* 19 (1972) 38–64.

13. For the general argumentation on this type of formation to

discipleship, see M. Hengel, *Nachfolge und Charisma* (Berlin: Töpelmann, 1968) 41–63; esp. 59–60.

14. For a discussion of the possible meanings, see I. H. Marshall, *Commentary on Luke* (Grand Rapids: Eerdmans, 1978) 898–99.

15. See *On Becoming a Catholic* 37–60, esp. 49–54.

16. For the rich biblical tradition behind this Pauline saying, see B. Rigaux,*Les Epîtres aux Thessaloniciens* (Paris: Gabalda, 1956) 374–79.

17. I. P. Ellis, " 'But Some Doubted'," *New Testament Studies* 14 (1967–68) 574–80; here, 576.

18. For a similar usage in Matt 28:17, as well as the connection between "falter" and "worship" in both pericopes, see *ibid.* 577–79; also, Meier, *The Vision of Matthew*, 98–100, 211–12.

19. A typical sociological discussion, for example, focuses on how a group socializes its converts; see T. E. Long and J. K. Hadden, "Religious Conversion and the Concept of Socialization," (see n. 3). A more interesting question that is outside the scope of our topic is how conversion might affect the development of community from an anthropological viewpoint; see P. R. Turner, "Religious Conversion and Community Development," *Journal for the Scientific Study of Religion* 18 (1979) 252–60.

20. See, e.g., R. M. Moseley, "Faith Development and Conversion in the Catechumenate," R. Duggan, ed., *Conversion and the Catechumenate*, 145–63.

21. See D. Senior and C. Stuhlmueller, *The Biblical Foundations of Mission* (Maryknoll, N.Y.: Orbis, 1983) esp. 262ff., 272ff., 299ff., 318ff.; F. Hahn, *Mission in the New Testament* (Naperville, Ill.: A. Allenson, 1965) 137–52.

22. *Religion and Alienation*, 200.

23. See the excellent systematic discussion of the mission of the Church in F. S. Fiorenza, *Foundational Theology. Jesus and the Church* (New York: Crossroad, 1984) 197–245.

24. As I have done so frequently in other writings, I refer particularly to the implications of R. M. Kanter, *Commitment and Community. Communes and Utopias in Sociological Perspective* (Cambridge: Harvard University, 1972).

25. I have discussed this within terms of life-stage studies in *Real Presence. Worship Sacraments, and Commitment* (San Francisco: Harper & Row, 1982).

26. See S. Crites, "The Narrative Quality of Experience," *Journal of the American Academy of Religion* 39 (1971) 291–311; M. Golberg, *Theology and Narrative* (Nashville: Abingdon, 1982); J. M. McClendon, *Biography as Theology* (Nashville: Abingdon, 1974).

27. See R. Schnackenburg, *Present and Future Modern Aspects of New Testament Theology* (Notre Dame: University of Notre Dame, 1966) 122–42.

28. Täglich Sterben und Auferstehen: Der Literalsinn von 2 Kor 4, 12–5, 10 (Munich: Kösel, 1973) 49–51; 51–58 provides an illuminating set of charts that outline these developments in Paul's writings.

29. *The Transformation of Man* (Springfield, Ill.: Templegate, 1967) 263.

30. *Letter to Pilgrims. A Commentary on the Epistle to the Hebrews* (New York: Pilgrim Press, 1981) 173; see also, *ibid.* 173–78; see also, J. Schreiner, "Führung–Thema der Heilsgeschichte im Alten Testament," *Biblische Zeitschrift* 5 (1961) 2–18.

31. For a fuller treatment of this argument, see my *On Becoming a Catholic* and *A Roman Catholic Theology of Pastoral Care* (Philadelphia: Fortress, 1983).

The Process of Conversion

2

The Process of Conversion

BARBARA O'DEA, D.W.

Conversion-talk is relatively new in the contemporary Catholic Church. Its language has a strange and somewhat threatening ring to American Catholic ears. That is hardly surprising. We are a Church who for centuries have believed that conversion is for others: for far-off people we labelled "pagan," for the unbaptized everywhere, and, closer to home for Protestants, too often regarded more as adversaries than as brothers and sisters in Christian faith. Perhaps today we might add to the 'to-be-converted' list the neo-pagan generation brought up in the shadow of the bomb. These are the people called to conversion. We, on the other hand, have already been baptized into the one true faith. The sense that the gospel call to conversion might also be directed to us is a Johnny-come-lately for most contemporary Catholics.

Moreover, we are a Church in which long ago the "faithful" became the "laity," those on the outer rim of Church life. Laity were the spectators, while pope, bishops, priests, and religious were the actors. How can we be expected to undergo the corporate transformation that will shift our horizons from a Church that is "them" to one that is "us"?

If conversion-talk is rare in our Church, rarer still is kingdom-talk. In fact, it has a fairy tale ring to our ears. As Americans, we are a pragmatic people who deal with the realities of our situation, not visionaries dreaming of a kingdom yet to come. To further complicate our situation, we belong to a nation built on the principle of separation of Church and State. As a people, we have worked hard to maintain that separation. Talk of "spreading the kingdom" leaves us feeling uncomfortable and turned off.

Finally, as American Catholics, we have been taught that religion and politics should not be mixed. We expect our bishops to speak out on the internal affairs of the Church while our government looks to our interests as a nation. What could it possibly mean for us to be a kingdom-people in the twentieth-century U.S.A.?

The effects of this experience are evident in all facets of our lives—personally and corporately. For the most part, as American Catholics, we live our lives in two worlds: the world of the sacred which we enter on Sunday morning and the secular world where we dwell the rest of the week. Kingdom-vision, gospel values, Christian identity are not terms in which we think and act. The values, moral standards, level of commitment evidenced in our daily lives differ only slightly from those of our secular contemporaries. Often our schizophrenia lies so deep that unconsciously we totally separate our individual and family lives from our broader communal and corporate involvements. Concern for life, for the equitable sharing of the goods of the earth, for ecology, for an end to the nuclear arms race, for peace, and for the future of our planet are not hallmarks of Catholic Christians in today's world.

Busy people in a busy world, we are activity-rich and experience-poor. We muddle through the crisis and conflicts in life that arise from relationships, from vocational commitments, from work situations, from church or other memberships. In the process we win some and we lose some. Many of us neither reflect on nor trust our experience a great deal. The price paid for lack of reflection is surface living. We are often unable to recognize the occasions for the kind of transforming growth that is conversion.

And our Church offers precious little to help us out of this quagmire. Liturgies intended to transform us through encounter with God often prevent it. Too many empty rituals placate our sense of obligation to worship God while at the same time shielding us from any more reality than we care to acknowledge. Still, the ritual itself survives— repeated weekly even daily in our churches.

Nor does the state of preaching help. Its content is often more doctrinal than scriptural; more intellectual than experiential; more didactic than challenging. Too many of us listen, week after week, to homilies that call us to little or nothing. As a result our sacramental celebrations do not adequately express the continuous transforming action of God in our lives. In fact, most of us are totally unaware that our Sunday liturgy is in any way connected to the renewal and deepening of our Christian commitment in baptism.

That conversion is a concern in this context is already a sign of the activity of the Spirit in our midst. In response, it is important that as Catholics we deepen our understanding of the conversion process. In approaching this topic I would like to raise three questions. On a personal level: what are the elements of the process of conversion? From a communal perspective: what does the Church have to offer persons on the journey of conversion? Finally, what are some implications of a conversion-oriented theology for the contemporary Church?

Personal Dimension

Rosemary Haughton describes conversion as a transformation of horizons[1] that effects the way a person envisions self, others and the world. It is a profoundly human experience. We have only to consider persons like Ghandi, Anwahr Sadat, or Dag Hammerskjold to realize that. It is important to keep this perspective in mind. Otherwise, in narrowing the phenomenon to a process which originates, unfolds, and comes to its conclusion uniquely in a Christian setting, we fail to observe the dramatic action of the Creator throughout the entire human family.

Conversion is a complex event. A given conversion experience may involve any or all of the following:[2]

- moral conversion—integration of the values one affirms into the way one lives;
- intellectual conversion—toward a holistic understanding of truth and human wisdom;
- religious conversion—recognition of the Mystery in life and turning towards the Holy;
- Christian conversion—turning to Jesus as the Christ and to the kingdom inaugurated by his coming;
- ecclesial conversion—turning to Church as the community which proclaims faith in the Mystery of God and in Jesus Christ.

All of these levels of conversion combine to make up a total conversion event. However, in reality human conversion experiences are always partial. Some may undergo a major theistic conversion that has no specific Christian dimension. Others, and many Catholics among them, may move through a process of turning towards Christ with only a minimal perception of the complementary ecclesial conversion that brings one into a sense of solidarity with all members of the Christ.

Since even major conversion experiences are incomplete, conversion is an ongoing process. To live in a state of readiness for and openness to the action of the Spirit within life experience is a lifelong task.

With these things in mind let us review the elements of the process of conversion. To accomplish this I have chosen the framework of a story. It is an x-ray approach, a picture of the skeletal components.[3] Ultimately it is in the language of story that we relate experiences of conversion and because it is in the paradigmatic stories of Scripture that we find the likeness between God's action in our personal story and in that of God's people throughout salvation history. There are five components in every good story: relative paradise, crisis, descent into hell, turning point and homecoming.

Relative paradise

Every good story begins in Eden. "Once upon a time there was . . . ." (In real life stories it is only a relative paradise, since people, and indeed all of creation are struggling towards fulfillment.) Nevertheless, the beginning of a story describes a time of relative stability, a "plateau" stage in life. It is a time when one's self-image, relationships, job, faith, life, place in the world all seem "right." One assumes that life is meant to be this way and will ever be thus.

Crisis

Inevitably, the scene begins to change. The turning point may come about imperceptibly in the inner world where crucial shifts begin. It may be brought to consciousness in a moment of quiet reflection or in a conversation with a friend. Or, crisis may be precipitated by traumatic encounters with illness or death, with prejudice or poverty. Levinson calls such happenings "marker events." They signal and precipitate turning points in one's life journey.

At this stage of the story the inner movement shifts from contentment to restlessness. Several points are noteworthy in a crisis stage: first, movement through the crisis and turning points in life do not in and of themselves constitute conversion. Rather, in Mark Searle's terms, conversion consists "in successful negotiation of crisis or change . . . ." It "is a form of 'passage' or 'transition' whereby a person *may* pass to a new set of relationships with self, the world around him (her) and with life itself."[4] Creative movement through periods of change is never automatic.

Second, crisis situations are times when one feels that life has gotten out of control. One is losing ground. The person does not choose the crisis, but rather is launched into it by the circumstances and events of life.

Finally, whether arising from within or without, the crisis affects one's whole world. Life begins to crumble. Even the vaguest consciousness that one is on the verge of significant change is fraught with a sense of danger. There is loss of meaning. Old assumptions are questioned, self-doubt and fear creep in. One begins to feel different, somewhat alienated from oneself, from life as one had known it, perhaps even from relationships.[5]

Gail Sheehy points out that during significant life passages there is an altered sense of time.[6] At the crisis stage, the subject of the story seems to be on a treadmill not able to advance, while time is slipping away. The journeyer is caught between longing for the good old days and an inner turmoil that impels him/her to move on. The dilemma at such moments is that there is no standing still. One is faced with a choice either to regress or to move forward. One can either deny the significance of life events and attempt to return to a previous stage or face the reality of one's circumstances and enter into the struggle that will precipitate one on towards transformation. This initial decision is not made easily. However, if the crisis is to be lived creatively, one must decide to face it.

Our faith tradition offers stories of conversion journeys. The most frequently cited is a gospel story which traces the journey from unbelief to faith in the Lord Jesus. It is the story of the disciples on the road to Emmaus. In tracing the elements of conversion, I would like to use a story from the Hebrew Scriptures which highlights a neglected aspect of conversion: the corporate dimension. For, as Christians, we are called to a common conversion, a common faith, a common vocation. The story is a tale of epic proportions, it describes a people's passage from slavery to freedom in response to God's call in their lives. It is the Exodus story. In it the crisis moment comes when the Hebrew people, faced by an event in their life history, must choose whether or not to leave the familiar land of Egypt for a destination unknown. Only those who took the risk were part of the forward movement of salvation history. Undoubtedly, there were others who, too frightened of very real dangers involved, chose not to move onward but to remain enslaved body and soul in Egypt.

Descent into Hell

The third moment in a story is relative hell. It is the point of no return when the actor feels powerless. There is a sense of being trapped on the horns of a dilemma. It is the moment of total darkness.

The choice may be between continuing to endure a difficult family relationship or facing the problem with little hope of a favorable outcome. It might be between remaining in one's hometown surrounded by family and friends or moving to a far away city to accept a better position. Struggle gives way to a sense of paralysis, of being unwilling or unable to decide. The person does not know which way to turn.

At this point, one feels too numb to grieve, too frightened to act, too lost to move. Time seems to stand still. Life, i.e., a life worth living, appears to be a thing of the past. It is a moment of discovery of one's weaknesses and needs, of one's selfishness and limitations.

The choice at this stage is between control and surrender. Where the movement is towards faith, it becomes a question of striving to "play God" in one's own life, or to surrender to the mysterious action of God.

This is the moment in the Exodus story when the Israelites, having set out on the journey, found themselves trapped between the Red Sea ahead and Pharaoh's pursuing army behind. There is no way out.

Turning Point

The catalyst which precipitates a breakthrough in the story is the surrender to Life. Once the person surrenders to the truth that is present in the experience, energy is released. The truth that one has received is related to the conflicts, questions and needs of the person involved.

For example, the man or woman who comes to admit in naked truth, "I am in need of help, I am an alcoholic," can begin to look at options for turning his/her life around, to recognize the people who are willing to help, the many others who share this disease, the friends and family members who rejoice ever so cautiously but hopefully that the corner has been turned.

At this point, for the subject there is a feeling of having dropped an immense burden, a sense of release, relief, freedom. Little by little one begins to look at life again, to take a few faltering steps in a new direction. There is a sense of smallness here, one knows one's weaknesses, has experienced one's boundaries and limitations. But in the process hidden resources have been discovered, untapped potential called forth. One begins to look forward.

The decision made, healthy fear remains; however, it is no longer the terror of meaninglessness. Seeds of hope are taking root. Within the person there is a dawning sense of the convergence of vision and values. There is light at the end of the tunnel. This is the moment to begin to live the new vision, to try new behaviors, to relate differently with others based on change that has taken place from the inside out.

For those moving towards Christian conversion and faith the decision is to a radical turning towards God and towards a new way of living based on gospel values. For others undergoing what Paul Robb, S.J., calls a second religious conversion,[7] the call is to transcend previous levels of faith and love, to move towards mature faith that transforms one from disciple to steward ready to invest oneself wholeheartedly in the mission of Christ.

In Exodus terms it is the moment of the parting of the waters and the passage through the Red Sea into a new land; a land of freedom from slavery. But this land is a desert wasteland where the Hebrews would begin to unravel the implications of the journey undertaken and discover the road that still lay ahead.

Homecoming

The final stage of our story corresponds to the final phase of many a good story "and they lived happily ever after" (. . . until the next turning point). It corresponds to those moments in life when there is a sense of a new synthesis. "The strife is o'er, the victory won." The passage has been completed, the vision transformed. There is a sense of wholeness and renewal manifested in feelings of "at-one-ment," of deep integration. One experiences a sense of homecoming. This is a time to unravel the implications of the vision and values that are the outcome of the passage successfully negotiated. At one with self, with others and with the ultimate reality of God, one is ready to reach out and take on the world. Time flies during such periods. There is so much one would like to do and so little time to accomplish it all.

In Exodus terms, the Hebrews have reached the promised land. In the Sinai covenant they have received a new identity. They are the People of God. Having passed through the Jordan, they have been given a new home, a land flowing with milk and honey. What that implies, they have yet to learn.

Communal Dimension

For some the search for meaning leads to questions of God and/or of Jesus. For those who choose to continue their search with others within the Church, several significant dimensions are added to the process and dynamics of conversion just outlined. I would like to say a word about three: tradition, community, and ritual.

Tradition

Adults who come to the Church to seek the meaning of their conversion journey bring a wealth of experience. To them the community offers the mirror of Scripture and the store of the accumulated wisdom which is its core tradition. There, seekers can discover their own story. They can begin to identify Exodus from slavery to freedom, passages through death to life with the mythic stories of passage in the Scriptures. In addition, tales of the procession of saints demonstrate the conviction and the fidelity of those who have gone before us in the faith. The stories of our faith tradition encourage newcomers to become one with believers who today have discovered Jesus to be the Way, the Truth, and the Life. Gradually, searchers are able to discern God's continuing presence and action in their own life story and in those of contemporary Church members.

It is in handing on the treasures of Scripture and the core tradition that Church teachings, rituals, and laws are rooted in the lives of people past and present. In this way, as Jim Dunning points out, doctrines, rituals, and commandments become part of the very identity of the believer. Doctrines are the very expression of what we believe, rituals are the expression of the way we worship, and the commandments are the expression of what we value.[8]

Community

The second significant dimension offered by the Church to the seeker is community. Here I am speaking about community in the sense of the Church as a community in progress towards the kingdom.[9] The gospel way is a collective way. Church communities, or more precisely core groups of believers within the larger structure, have an awareness of their *identity* as the Body of Christ and a consciousness of their *mission* to spread the values of the Kingdom of God in the contemporary world.

For people experiencing conversion passages, initiating parish communities provide continuity in the midst of discontinuity. They offer hospitality during a time of alienation as they welcome the searcher. They bring companionship in a time of loneliness as they join others and walk with them. They are light in a time of darkness as they share their own stories of struggle and doubt of peace and conviction. It is the community members who invite and foster a sense of belonging as they hand on the treasures of the faith. Witnesses communicate the vision of what it means to live one's baptismal vocation in the family, in the workplace, and in society. Finally, it is the community that ritualizes the experiences of conversion thus affirming that what is happening in the life of the seeker is good, meaningful, and necessary for the growth of the person and of the Church.

Ritual

The third dimension which the Church offers is ritual. Symbol is the vehicle of expression of that which is beyond all telling, the language of mystery, the medium of encounter with the holy. It is the language of ritual in which the person can be brought into a liminal state where there is room for an experience of the transcendent.

Ritual activity fosters encounter with the holy to the extent that participants are brought into touch with the archetypal experience which is the source of their common identity and purpose. In the liturgy the Church expresses the experience of God shared by its members in a ritual framework. Committed to dying and rising with Christ, believers assemble to hear the Word of faith that brings meaning to their experience and to enter into the transforming encounter with Christ in sacrament. The love of God poured forth in Christ is received as a timeless, total gift. The response to that love is dying, a surrender that leaves behind all cautions. In surrender, the person finds meaning and newness of life.

Ritual provides the setting for the deepening of the believer's conversion and commitment while at the same time bonding him or her to community members through the celebration of common faith and the renewal of a common covenant.

Mark Searle summarizes this potential of liturgy. He says: "Every liturgical celebration of the Church . . . is an attempt to facilitate the experience of conversion by ritualizing it. . . . Every sacrament is a rite of passage:

it is an opportunity to live through the transition occurring within our own lives in explicit identification with the passage of Jesus through death . . . to the Father."[10]

The tremendous influence of these three treasures: tradition, community and ritual, offered by the Church to a person in the midst of the conversion journey are sometimes overlooked, never overestimated.

Implications

One of the major contributions of the RCIA in the contemporary Church is its renewed focus on conversion. Because conversion is the cornerstone of faith, every other dimension of Christian life must be shifted and realigned with this foundation. The resulting perspective will require dramatic changes in outlook and praxis. I would like to state five basic implications of a conversion-oriented theology and note some challenges.

Restoration of a Kingdom-Vision

In a Christian context focus on conversion requires restoration of a kingdom-vision. Christian conversion is a fundamental reorientation of one's whole life in line with the vision and values of the Kingdom of God.

The Kingdom of God must come to be recognized in the world wherever signs of the transforming action of God are present. Wherever people are feeding the world's hungry, healing their wounds, proclaiming truth and justice, striving for peace, there is the Kingdom of God. In this perspective it must become clear to Catholics that the Kingdom of God is not co-extensive with the Church. Rather, within the human family the Church is called to *recognize* the seeds of the kingdom. Christians are called to collaborate with all who are working to cultivate and spread the values of the Kingdom in the world. Only when our horizons are broadened to recognize God's Presence in the whole of creation will it be possible to envision social conversion of global dimensions.

Starting Point and Condition of Christian Discipleship

Conversion must be understood as the starting point and the condition of Christian discipleship. The call of Jesus in the Gospels is to "Repent (Meta/Noein) and believe the Good News." Metanoia involves an inward dimension: a change of mind and change of heart through which the values of the kingdom Jesus preached gradually become our own. But metanoia cannot be limited to inner change. One cannot claim to turn to the Lord without turning towards the Kingdom of God in the world. Christian conversion must be seen as multi-dimensional. It involves *faith*, i.e., a personal commitment to Jesus as Lord. It involves *community*, i.e., communion with all who believe in Christ, a sense of universality, a world Church. It involves *mission*, i.e., participation in the baptismal vocation of the Church to live gospel values and spread the Good News.

Starting Point for Pastoral Ministries

Because it is a primary focus for the encounter with God, human experience must become the starting point for pastoral ministries. Both the basic formation of catechumens and the formation involved in the development of mature Christian spirituality must begin with people's experience, lead them to value that experience, and help them to recognize the call of God within that experience.

A corollary is that Church ministers must become skilled in enabling persons and parish communities to discern God's call in the personal and social dimensions of contemporary life. In particular, preaching and catechesis must draw upon contemporary experience. They must enable catechumens and faithful to name their experience and to recognize its reflection in the stories of Scripture thus bonding them to all who have followed Christ throughout the ages.

Corporate Ecclesial Conversion

Catholics must be called to corporate ecclesial conversion. As a result of reflection on the Church in the modern world, the bishops at Vatican II called for what amounts to a major paradigmatic shift in our understanding of Church. Suddenly, Catholics were asked to make a 180° turn and transform their vision of the Church:

From:	*To:*
Church as hierarchy (them)	Church as People of God (us)
Church as a haven of salvation (enclave)	Church in the world (mission)

While the vision is integrative, appealing, and more true to the life situation of believers, it calls for an ecclesial conversion of universal proportions. One of the major obstacles to internalizing the ecclesial vision of Vatican II is that Catholic people were given the product without the process. The prior formation necessary to open people to the potentially transforming vision as well as the subsequent formation necessary to assist them to understand it must be provided.

Baptism as a Vocation

Catholics must come to recognize baptism as a vocation. A growing number of Catholics who have experienced renewal through participation in catechumenal ministries or in renewal movements have voiced regret that they have never had the same opportunities as the catechumens in their parishes. A few even inquire about the possibility of rebaptism. The desire indicated by these comments should not be taken lightly.

Catholics must be called to recognize that baptism is both an event and a vocation. It is the symbolization of incorporation into the Kingdom. Growing into our baptism, i.e., becoming people who embody the vision and values of the Kingdom is a lifetime process. Conversion and faith must involve the believer in a continuing process of changing his/her vision and way of life. Catholics must be helped to understand that one cannot be a disciple if one already knows all the answers. Moreover, to keep on repeating the same answers is to stifle the power of the gospel. They must hear the Good News that baptism is a way of life. Conversion and the faith that is a response to conversion are activities rather than states.

In conclusion, allow me to offer some practical challenges for the immediate future.

Clergy, realize that in the Catholic Church, for better or for worse, you have enormous power to shape the vision and values of the faithful. Bishops and priests, realize the impact of your leadership style. Know that enablement of the faithful deserves high priority on your scale of investment of time and energy.

Homilists, help those of us who listen to you week after week to claim our call to conversion. Preach it to us in season and out in a manner that is more experiential than intellectual, more scriptural than doctrinal, more challenging than didactic. Help us to name the personal and especially the corporate roadblocks on our conversion journey. And, if you are going to preach conversion to us, you must model it for us.

Religious educators, use sound androgogical approaches

with us. Call upon our experience and hold up to us the mirrors of scripture and tradition that we may be rooted and founded in Christ. Help us to reshape our vision of Church and kingdom. Proclaim, repeat, insist that personal commitment and active involvement in mission are hallmarks of mature Christians.

Liturgists, lead us on our inward journey. Open us to the formative myths that are the very heart of our reality as Church. Help us to realize how the Exodus and the Paschal Mystery continue to answer symbolically the great questions of the human condition—questions of life and death, of suffering, of God, and of the meaning of the world. Only then can we discover meaning in them and live out of them on our life journey.

Finally, all pastoral ministers, devote resources of personnel, time, energy, funds to programs and experiences which raise parishioners consciousness of their vocation to collaborate in spreading the values of the kingdom through their lives in the marketplace.

If these efforts are successful, the next generation will be able to proclaim that the foundations have been laid. Conversion-talk and kingdom-talk will be familiar in Catholic parishes. The challenge that remains will be to deepen and live the vision.

Notes

1. Rosemary Haughton, *The Transformation of Man* (New York: Paulist, 1967) 7.
2. Edward K. Braxton, "Dynamics of Conversion" in *Conversion and the Catechumenate* (New York: Paulist, 1984) 111–17.
3. For a systematic approach to the process of conversion through the medium of story, cf. *Stories of Faith*, John Shea (Chicago: Thomas More, 1980).

4. Mark Searle, "The Journey of Conversion," *Worship* 54, no. 1 (January 1980) 36.
5. For an elaboration of the characteristics of the crisis experience, cf. Searle's article, 37-42.
6. Gail Sheehy, *Passages*. Predictable Crisis in Adult Life (New York: Dutton, 1976) 30.
7. Paul V. Robb, "Conversion as a Human Experience," *Studies in the Spirituality of Jesuits* XIV, no. 3 (May 1982) 7.
8. James B. Dunning, "The Stages of Initiation: 1. Inquiry," *Becoming a Catholic Christian* (New York: Sadlier, 1978) 94.
9. The intrinsic relationship between conversion, kingdom and Church in the Scriptures is explored in *The Call to Conversion* by Jim Wallis (San Francisco: Harper & Row, 1981).
10. Searle, *The Journey of Conversion* 49.

*Conversion and the Rite of
Christian Initiation of Adults*

3

Conversion and the Rite of Christian Initiation of Adults

JAMES D. SHAUGHNESSY

I welcome with enthusiasm the topic assigned to me for this meeting. If I were privileged to select my own topic, I could not have chosen one more compatible with my appraisal of the needs of the Church in our time or more representative of the convictions I have developed over a period of time reaching beyond the reemergence of the Rite of Christian Initiation of Adults and the Council that produced it.

It has been a long-standing conviction of mine that, to no small degree, many of the problems we face in our pastoral ministry today stem directly from our misunderstanding of or our failure to appreciate the proper function and importance of baptism as it relates to our lives as a community of baptized believers. That we most often fall short in the execution of our ministries because the causal relationship between baptism and Christian discipleship is not adequately understood.

Anthropologists tell us that great insights can be gained into the life of a people, tribe, or nation by the way they initiate their neophytes and bury their dead. A most casual appraisal using this criterion should tell us that as Christians we are in deep trouble. The cavalier fashion in which we have been initiating new members and the nearly total abdication of responsibility for the burial of our dead should give us serious pause.

Given these circumstances, there should be no wonderment that the RCIA has struck a responsive chord in the hearts of those with even limited insight into the real state of the pastoral scene. In the mind of this assembly, there should be no question that the restoration of Christian initiation of adults provides us with a most valuable tool to begin the process of the reform of our faith communities and eventually the Church in our time.

An Ecclesial Perspective

My basic assumption is this: everything we are and everything we do as baptized believers, whether it be in community or as individuals, should be viewed in terms of what we are as Church. This may be expressed in many different ways with each nuanced distinction adding a richness to our appreciation of who we are and the task we take up. We are the gathered community of Christ's disciples, an assembly of God's People present to the world, a people called to witness to the Good News of salvation. In this light we must be Church, "the gathered," in the richest sense of that term, for we are being called into being through a faith-gifted response to the Good News. We are brought to reality through Christian initiation whose rich and normative form is adult initiation celebrated in the full panoply of all its elements stretching from pre-evangelization through the successive states and periods of the RCIA, to mystagogia and an evolving life commitment to God and neighbor. Furthermore, the more present and constant this initiatory celebration is to this faith community, and the more involved and open-ended their participation and concomitant conversion, the greater is the possibility that the will of Christ may come to fulfillment in the lives of such a community of disciples.

Before we address the central theme of this paper, there are some minor housekeeping chores that we must attend to as prologue. This is done to set forth the context out of which I intend to draw my conclusions and state my case.

Liturgical Renewal: An Unfinished Task

The past four or five decades have been, in terms of the liturgical and spiritual life of the gathered believers, as exciting and challenging as any previous or equivalent period in history. Still, there is a caution here. Because most of us have been so closely and so intimately involved in many aspects of this action, and because the tempest has (at times) been so fierce, it is difficult to sort out much of what has taken place and, more importantly, to evaluate the real worth and lasting effects of what has transpired. The task becomes ever more challenging as we attempt to plot a future course and prepare to use efficiently the many tools provided us, particularly the excellent tool we find in the RCIA.

At the outset I wish to state clearly something that many of us have known or felt for a long time and about which some have been more or less vocal. There has not been the progress many seem to think; we have further to go than most are willing to admit; few have been either as knowledgeable, vocal, or active as they might or should have been. I am further convinced that what our time needs is a real, full-blown, twentieth-century Jeremiah, someone who will tell us how it is and what we ought to do about it in clear and certain terms. I hope it is not cowardice that prompts me to state that I feel neither called nor qualified.

In spite of all the reform and renewal that has taken place in our time, (particularly such recent examples as the unprecedented expansion of our liturgical library— Sacramentary, Lectionary, Ritual, and Breviary; the veritable explosion in liturgical studies and sister sciences; an ever increasing number of trained and educated personnel; stronger and more effective international, national, and regional associations and academies; a hierarchy more favorably disposed to the need and the urgency to devote more time, personnel and funds to the cause), the plain and observable fact is that we are still light-years away from our stated goal. Although some have heard the message and are responding well, there are many others who, if they have heard the message, give little evidence of responding. The difficulty is no longer aggressive and resolute opposition. I sometimes wish it were. In such circumstances we could identify the enemy and engage them in contest. A great deal of what we face today is a vast shift in priorities that finds expression in both word and attitude that liturgy is NOT ". . . a sacred action surpassing all others (or that) no other action of the Church can equal its efficacy by the same title and to the same degree." [1] The term for this malaise is apathy.

It is my purpose to be as positive and constructive as possible as I attempt to identify some of the areas in which we are falling short of our potential and to which we must address ourselves if we have any intention to make progress toward the goal of vital faith communities firmly on their pilgrim way to the Kingdom. This is a project that should be preceded and accompanied by critical analysis of the real situation confronting us, while we remain convinced that the goal is achievable, not visionary.

A Holistic Approach

Because I consider the Church to be an integral whole, greater than the sum of its parts, my approach will be holistic to the degree that I find that possible. Although there are numerous New Testament ecclesiologies and although we find no uniform or monolithic structure in the New Testament, yet when we find the Church described as the People of God, the Body of Christ, our concept of the Church gives clear evidence of a corporate personality, a oneness in Christ. In baptism we are made one with Christ, dead and risen, and with and in one another. In post-baptismal chrismation our baptism is perfected in the Spirit. In the Eucharist this unity is sustained as we live and make present in the world the God who justifies and brings salvation.

As I deal with the RCIA, I want to make it clear that the RCIA does not, nor is it intended to, exist in isolation from all the other working elements of the community we call Church. Much less is it to become the dominant or sole activity of the community of disciples. The RCIA is a tool, albeit an excellent one; it is not magic but a splendid means that, when properly used and understood, can contribute much to the growth and development of the community of believers. A smooth blending and integration into the total pastoral mission or apostolate is the proper function of the RCIA.

It is my confirmed opinion that we must not consider the RCIA without identifying its proper situs—the local Church, specifically the parish. To fail to do so could only lead to a distortion of the rite and a serious misuse of an excellent tool. Is it possible that we have been too euphoric about the prospects of the RCIA turning the Church around and solving our problems? That we have run ahead of ourselves while overlooking the bedrock foundation upon which and within which the RCIA must live, breathe, and bear fruit? For this reason it is my intention to ask you to pause a moment and give thought to two aspects of our lived-faith that we know are essential if we have any intention of being Church. How do we conceive the Church? How do we relate to Christ? It has been my experience that a great number of our people have undeveloped if not distorted or heavily structured institutional notions of Church and a concept of Christ that borders the pietistic. It is a further conviction that unless we clarify our thinking about these two essentials of our lived-faith and make them clear and evident in all our teaching, preaching, living, and witnessing, there is not going to be the growth and development in the Church we all desire and work so hard to bring forth in the lives of our faith communities.

What I am attempting to say is that there must be some very determined and well thought out efforts on our part as leaders in the area of pastoral ministry to integrate our entire ministry so that it is obvious to all who are willing and eager to see (and they are multitude) that we must view the Church holistically, integrate all that we do so that each aspect of our ministry clearly manifests the unity that is Christ and the Church. The malady we suffer is longstanding. It has led to the disintegration of several important elements of the sacramental system to the extent that we can and frequently do some very strange things with sacraments without being aware that what we do is at odds with the purpose of the sacraments and lacking continuity with the early Christian tradition of the Church that produced them.

Sacramental Implications

Several cases in point. With the RCIA we have started to move in a direction that may very well restore Christian initiation to its original sequence and purpose. The traditional sequence of baptism, post-baptismal anointing, and Eucharist is fairly well accepted and has priority of established position in the adult rite. But how long can we sustain the dichotomy of adult initiation going in one direction and the initiation of children in another? This schizophrenic approach to initiation cannot be productive. What is more disruptive, even dangerous, is an approach to Christian initiation that is more of the nature of initiating new members into the club, rather than of welcoming and nurturing disciples committed to Christ and of bringing them to maturity in Christ as their ministry evolves within and extends out from the faith community as mission.

In a similar vein, who is there who will rescue the sacrament of penance and reconciliation from the desuetude that threatens its very existence? Restore its real function as the "second plank of salvation" and the reconciliation of the faith community? The factors that contribute to this are many, and it is not the function of this paper to delineate them. Yet, in this vein, I would like to present an idea for your consideration. With respect to the sacrament of penance, we have so confused or failed to distinguish the practice of virtue of penance from the sacrament of penance. As a result we have overloaded the circuitry of the sacrament of penance with faults, misdemeanors, and other peccadillos which properly belong within the province of the virtue of penance. Thus the sacrament is placed in serious jeopardy. We have permitted the sacrament of penance to float in space, viewing it as a handy but isolated and individual tool of convenience. In doing so we have separated it from an integrated spiritual life while failing to acknowledge the distinction that must exist in knowing the relationship and interdependence of virtue and sacrament. We could go on with this discouraging story, but enough is enough. Unless and until such time as we begin to integrate the whole of our lives as community in Christ, we will fail to see the need for an integrated understanding of who we are and what we do as disciples of Christ committed to witness and mission.

The Church: A Community of Disciples

In the period immediately prior to Vatican Council II and since, we have experienced a number of attempts to find new ways to describe the Church in terms of models. All, more or less, depart from the concept of the Church as institutional and hierarchical in nature. Most have been helpful to the degree that they stimulated new ideas and challenged us to rethink our understanding of Church and how it should reflect the mission of Christ in a new time and age, while we abandon the alabaster monolith that dominated much of our past thinking.

One of the most effective of these authors has been Avery Dulles, first with his *Models of the Church* in the early seventies and then with his current effort *A Church to Believe In.* In the latter book Dulles puts it this way: "The Church is and must be *one.* To be an efficacious sign of God's redemptive work in Christ, it must be a fellowship of reconciliation; it must bring its members together into a community of faith, trust, and mutual concern, thus reversing the effects of human sin which has alienated people from God, from one another, and from themselves." [2]

Dulles tells us that it was a statement of Pope John Paul II in *Redemptor Hominis* that prompted him to use a new model—the Community of Disciples. The Pope states: "Membership in that (Mystical Body of Christ) has for its source a particular call, united with the saving action of grace. Therefore, if we wish to keep in mind this community of the People of God, which is so vast and so extremely differentiated, we must see, first and foremost, Christ saying in a way to each member of the community: 'Follow me.' It is the community of the disciples, each of whom in a different way—at times very consciously and consistently—is following Christ. This shows also the deeply 'personal' aspect and dimension of this society. . . ."[3]

It is in terms of this oneness in Christ and in each other expressed in the New Testament Church that I wish to consider the local faith community (the parish family) as the primary base in which and by means of which we function as baptized believers and into which we continue to grow by initiating new members. I am firmly convinced that the faith community as a vibrant, loving, and caring community is a vital link in the total initiation process. But more importantly, if such a family is not present, involved, and eager to accept and nourish the new Christians, we are in serious trouble.

The Spiritual Health of the Parish

Although the parish, as the matrix for the newly baptized believers, is not the main focus of this paper, I would consider myself derelict if I did not place in the forefront an appeal to all concerned with the Christian initiation of adults to keep the state of the parish, especially its spiritual health as community, uppermost in their minds while they spend themselves so profligately in the cause of Christian witness.

It is in the area of community building that the concept of wholeness becomes most evident. It has been my experience that all our attitudes, our efforts, the way we pray, the way we worship, the way we preach, the way we instruct, the way we approach people, the way we care and respond to their needs, as well as every other aspect of witness and mission should keep this concept of wholeness in the forefront of all planning and activities. Without such effort there will be little in the way of a parish "support group" to accept, much less to sustain to maturity, our new-born Christians.

This is where the RCIA and conversion come into the picture. It is my firm conviction that with the RCIA functioning at the best possible level in our parish communities and with a clearer concept and greater commitment to conversion properly understood, as well as open-ended all the way to the *Eschaton*, we have the most excellent of tools as we continue our task of building the kingdom on earth in anticipation of the final Kingdom.

Baptismal Growth

As we consider conversion in many of its various and significant manifestations, I must, at the outset, establish a "given" without which any proper understanding or appreciation of conversion becomes either impossible or illusory. This is that baptism is a permanent, vital, not static, dimension of Christian living. We must reject from the outset any idea that baptism may be regarded as the primary and indispensable condition of Christian life which, once established, may be progressively ignored as we grow in faith. Such a "once-and-forever" understanding of the state of the baptized, an understanding that has been rejected from the beginning, is more prevalent among us than most are aware. Note the warning in Heb 6:4–6: "It is impossible to restore again to repentance those who have once been enlightened." The consensus understanding of this passage is that "a constant state of *metanoia*" has always been a proper post-baptismal description of the vital and committed Christian. It must be clear therefore to all that our conversion is not complete this side of the *Parousia*.

Conversion within the Context of Baptism and Faith

Because my colleagues have dealt with the more basic and fundamental elements of conversion and conversion as process, I would like to address myself to conversion and the RCIA from the vantage point of one actively engaged in pastoral ministry.

In an essay appearing in volume 22 of *Concilium*, Hendrik Manders places the question of conversion within the context of baptism and faith. In so doing he relates conversion with the principles of the doctrine of justification, of sacraments, and God's saving Presence in the world. He focuses the issue by asking two questions. The first is "How do I find a merciful God?" The second is "How does God appear in this world through baptism (and) how does (this merciful God) become again a living God in baptism?"[4] These questions are vitally interdependent. It is important for us to be aware that it makes a great difference how we start with these questions and where we place the emphasis.

The question of Christian initiation and the conversion which accompanies it will be understood differently if we believe that it is the function of faith and baptism to uncover the deepest meaning of human existence. To discover self is to be infinitely involved in the conversion experience, and yet there is a great deal more to be discovered than self, regardless of how important we consider that to be. As believers we identify this greater discovery as the revelation of the divine reality of a saving God, a loving Father, who reveals himself and justifies us in and through his Divine Son and the Holy Spirit. Discovering and relating to the saving God and our neighbor is the prime object of Christian initiation.

Manders reiterates this point: "It makes a difference whether one thinks that grace is a purely immanent divine act and that, although it is a human reality, it is nevertheless essentially invisible and accessible only to the faith, or, whether one thinks that the incarnation of the Son of God implies essentially that grace becomes manifest in this world."[5] It is terribly important that we emphasize that it is a merciful God we discover through the initiation process, and that an open-ended and life commitment to this God in society through conversion is the ongoing vocation of all baptized believers.

Further Questions

But we must not stop there. We must posit further questions. How does God appear in the world in Christian initiation? How does God become again an evident and living God through baptism? How does grace become manifest in this world?

I understand this to mean that in Christian initiation there takes place an incarnation of sorts, an indwelling that becomes evident in action. We discover not only the merciful and forgiving God, but that in our act of dying and rising with Christ we become one with him as living members of his Body. As members of this Body we assume ministries in keeping with our graced capacities and opportunities, not least among these ministries is that of witness and responsibility to the society we call world. In our flesh we not only make up "what is lacking in the sufferings of Christ," but we also witness to the Good News of the gospel in the flesh and make Christ present to the world as we heal the sick, feed the hungry, clothe the naked, and shelter the homeless.

How do I find a merciful God? It is well to remind ourselves that this merciful God is not our private possession. We must share him, and although his mercy is spent profligately upon us, it must not end there. It is only to the degree that we receive mercy and forgiveness that we can be merciful and forgiving.

It is in this light that the second question concerning Presence really comes to life. "How does God appear through baptism? How does God appear in this world?"[6] It is in and through the baptized believers who have "seen" God, been touched by his mercy, tasted his sweet love, received and accepted his merciful forgiveness that God becomes visible in this world to all who have eyes to see and ears to hear and pain to be touched.

It is as old and as new as when Peter responded to the question: "And you, who do you say that I am?" "You are the Messiah, the Son of the living God." The Lord's reply puts it all in focus: "Blessed are you, Simon . . . . No mere man has revealed this to you, but my heavenly father" (Matt 16:17). I like to think that something very much like this happens to each of us, in our own degree, in our own time, as we progress to fuller responsibility for our baptismal commitment.

In theory it is relatively easy. The real task will be putting flesh and bone around these beliefs to give them life, make them visible, not so much in the world for that is too grand, too distant, but at arms length in our families, parish and otherwise, our neighborhoods (even if we live on the "right" side of the tracks), but always among the needy wherever they may be.

If we are to be responsible for the RCIA and the conversion it demands, and I am firmly convinced that we are, then we must be done with the idea that conversion is only for those who have not Christ. Granted there are the new and becoming converts in the process of conversion. But by far the greater number of persons in need of conversion are the vast horde of baptized believers who inhabit our parishes, who are in the process of forming the faith community.

Role of the Laity

The task is so vast that one could start almost any place. I would like to put the task in some relationship with what I consider the more important areas. One important area of great need is one we might call the "vocation syndrome." I am old enough to think of this in a religious context, but don't let that fool you. Although the so-called "shortage" creates some pain, I welcome it as an oracle of the Holy Spirit reminding us to rethink the real composition of the Church. It has always been true, but is now becoming painfully apparent to many, that the laity comprise the overwhelming portion of the Church, that we are not lacking in sufficient supply of proper ministers. It is just a matter of recognizing them, preparing them, permitting them to function to the fullest and at the highest degree of their competent ministries. The laity have always been the real strength of the Church. It is just a question of admitting it.

There is another great advantage in involving the laity. We frequently question the level of knowledgeable participation in communal prayer and worship: the laity seem to be uninvolved, distracted, and bored. What better way to elicit their active participation than to engage them in deeper and more demanding ministry on behalf of the total community at prayer? It will work. In so doing we not only gain ministers, but we develop a more informed and involved congregation, create better worship, and rescue our people from the Lord's Day blahs.

Pastoral Reflections

I would now like to go through the rite in a selective manner pointing out some thoughts that spring from my experience with the rite in a small, semi-intercity parish where the median age is in the mid-sixties and where the pace is pleasingly moderate. We usually have a few catechumens, but we have had years when there were no candidates for Christian initiation. Obviously this disturbed me for a number of reasons, the more important being that there would be no catechumenal exposure or participation within the community during the Lenten season, Holy Week, and that a prime element of the Vigil would be missing in a faith community where our Vigil begins at 8:00 p.m. and concludes with the Easter Eucharist at 6:00 a.m.

To supply for this considerable lacunae we did what we thought was the next best thing. We asked for volunteers from the parish (including cradle Catholics and adult converts recent and otherwise) to participate in a modified catechumenate that would be adapted to their needs and celebrated within the faith community. We have not had any outside objective analysis, but it was the unanimous conclusion of all who took part internally or externally that it was a success and well worth the effort. Each in their own way experienced growth and insights of faith in their spiritual life and its expression as a community of service. Because not a few of the participants were catechists and other ministers directly or indirectly related to the RCIA, it occurred to us that such an experience could be considered as a means of preparing members of the RCIA team. There is no substitute for personal experience.

It has been my experience that too many of us are still in the "mechanic" or "craft" stage of our development as far as many of the sacramental reforms are concerned. This is particularly true of the RCIA. There are exceptions, but too many have not yet emerged from the "show me how to do it" phase of Christian experience. We still have a great deal of "old baggage" to jettison before we can really come to grips with the essence of the total process of Christian initiation and the open-ended growth and development that must become a way of life. To cite a few examples that remain from the old "convert class" approach: the crass "sales pitch" approach to the pool of prospects; the cerebral as distinct from the experiential method of catechesis; an inability or unwillingness to clearly distinguish between the baptized and the unbaptized; the "end-of-the-road" concept of initiation that severely diminishes mystagogia or neglects it entirely; and perhaps the most menacing of all, the lack of a developed or developing faith community matrix so necessary to nurture the new Christian to maturity. To initiate neophytes and then abandon them to their own resorts is to act irresponsibly.

There is more that must be said. A thorough study of the document *Rite of Christian Initiation of Adults* in all its details, i.e., decree, introduction, and all the rites, must precede any "tinkering" with the document or adaptation of the rites. The adage "if it isn't broken, don't fix it" should be a primary criterion. Study it, live it, experience it, know it, and use it for at least a decade before tinkering with it.

Even in the best of circumstances, there are problems that involve more than the vastness and the mystery of the task itself. The classic in this respect is the question of evangelization and the precatechumenate. The entire matter of coming to faith is so personal, so individual, that anything that even intimates the "herd" approach must be thoroughly examined. Persons, circumstances, opportunities, motivation, practically everything involved in the process of embracing Christ is so diverse while remaining fiercely particular that there can hardly be such a thing as a standard program. Paul VI put it well when he said in reference to pastoral effectiveness in the ritual use of the sacraments: "The mysterious encounter between the divine, transcendent activity and a human, ministerial activity is something that deserves a continuous reflection, a wonderful rebirth, a constant vivid realization."[7] It is within this context that the vibrantly active faith community that prays, worships, lives, loves, and cares for others is so important as witness in the mission of the Church.

Once the decision is made that the inquirers have made sufficient progress "in the basic fundamentals of the spiritual life and Christian teaching . . . (and have evidenced) . . . initial conversion and desire . . . to enter into contact with God in Christ . . . ."[8] the rite of becoming a catechumen is celebrated within the assembly of the faith community and more active catechesis begins. Accepting and building on all that is contained in paragraphs 14 through 20 of the *Introduction* to the RCIA, I would like to relate our preference in "Word catechesis." After instruction and demonstration concerning the meaning and function of the liturgical year, I know of no better Word catechesis than that found in the Lectionary and the Breviary, that is, the concomitant daily readings from Scripture and the Fathers. Needless to say, this process is to be replete with examples, images, experiences from daily life, contact with the faith community, and all possible and conceivable ways and means to integrate the catechumens into their new community of faith. Such an approach not only introduces the candidates to the sequence of revealed faith in Christ and how to live it, but also familiarizes them with the basic library of Christian prayer and worship. This approach would also include prayers and readings from both the Sacramentary and Ritual as we demonstrate the part these essential books play in our lives as baptized believers. A word of caution here We must not presume that our people, much less our neophytes, know anything about the Church year. It is so removed from any concept they may have of the calendar year that more than a cursory introduction and instruction must be undertaken.

It should be obvious that the above program is to be intensified as we enter the period of purification and enlightenment with the rite of election and enrollment of names. There is also a greater contact with and involvement in the faith community, not only in its prayer and worship life but also the social implications of imaging Christ to our neighbor. Needless to say, there is an interaction here that is essential so as to renew . . . the community of the faithful.

We have also made what we consider to be a useful addition to the ceremonies of the presentations of the instruments of the faith (the Creed and the Lord's Prayer), that is the presentation of the book of the Scriptures. This presentation may be more meaningful and useful during the catechumenate than during the period of enlightenment, and although some decry it, we find it very helpful. It certainly has made an impressive impact on both the candidates and the faith community as we struggle to re-establish the Scriptures to their rightful place in the lives of the faithful.

The period of mystagogia is also in need of more thought and adaptation, not only in the area of mystagogical catechesis but also with respect to how we integrate and sustain the neophytes. Catechesis can well be continued at the level of the Word with the use of the seasonal readings and prayers found in the Lectionary, Sacramentary, and Breviary. The matter of integration once more accentuates the crying need for genuine faith communities who know who and what they are, and how they are to function, not only at prayer, worship, and celebration, but in every facet of their lived Christianity. Committed Christians who have their wings out for all who need them in any way, whoever they might be. And this need is particularly true of the neophyte.

There is also a great need to rethink the problem we face with respect to the baptized and the non-baptized seeker. There must be some way in which we can integrate them and at the same time honor the unmistakeable fact that there is an essential difference between the baptized and the unbaptized. In many respects this difference requires that their different status be acknowledged and dealt with accordingly.

Notes

1. Constitution on the Sacred Liturgy, *Sacrosanctum Concilium* Art. 7, *Documents on the Liturgy* (Collegeville: The Liturgical Press, 1982) 6.
2. Avery Dulles, *A Church to Believe In* (New York: Crossroads, 1983) 49.
3. *Ibid.* 7.
4. Hendrik Manders, "The Relation between Baptism and Faith," in *Concilium: Adult Baptism and the Catechumenate* (New York: Paulist, 1967) 4.
5. *Ibid.* 4–5.
6. *Ibid.* 4.
7. Paul VI, Address to a meeting of the presbyterate of Rome on pastoral effectiveness in the ritual use of the sacraments, October 29, 1970, *Notitiae* 6 (1970) 337–79. *Documents on the Liturgy* (Collegeville: The Liturgical Press, 1982) 712.
8. Christian Initiation of Adults, Introduction, art. 15, *Documents on the Liturgy* (Collegeville: The Liturgical Press, 1982) par. 2342, 738.

Visions and Challenges

4

Visions and Challenges

JAMES LOPRESTI, S.J.

Visions of the road ahead are not hard to come by. We might even say that too many people have too many of them. And while too many prophets may well spoil the view with the clutter of their predictions, even more hazardous is the situation of people with visions also being the people with the power to hasten their realization. Not every vision is true, valuable, or even worthy. The American dream, for example, has become the third world's nightmare, and futurists with too much power become the Big Brothers of society. No, seeing the future and making it happen is probably less urgent than not seeing the future and still hoping for the elusive kingdom. It was what the two disciples on the way to Emmaus couldn't yet see that saved them. It is our corporate Emmaus walk, if you will, that we must make together.

Challenges are another matter. They are the raw material of human life. They keep it moving. If I may borrow from da Vinci, human life is like water; immobility corrupts it! On the other hand, the flow of human life changes may either nurture us in refreshing newness or overwhelm us in the destructive flood. We need wisdom to know which kind is coming around the bend in the river and decide how to deal with it. All this week as we have been talking about conversion, we have been considering something which is the subset of the larger issue, i.e., change. Conversion has to do with our response to, acceptance of, dealing with, the demands of change, the successful negotiation of change, as Barbara O'Dea mentioned. Conversion, when it is truly life directed, has to do with the right attitude about, and the integration of, the changes which life serves up. It is a feature of human flexibility and tenacity in right relationship. Changed circumstances meet human life and say "deal with me." Conversion requires a deep seated, truthful response to that challenge. It is made up of assent to the truth and consent to its demands. Different from Snoopy's experience, it means having the ability to suffer consequences.

So I do not intend to offer much in the way of new visions, like a liturgical Jeanne Dixon, but I do have something to say about challenge, in particular about the flow of changes I think we need to be ready for, both personally and, more especially, as a people with responsibility for a community's corporate life. We're talking about institutional conversion, if you will.

Human change, in response to the challenge of truth, like the changes of any organism or organic system, happens in fits and starts, forward and backward, energy surge and energy conservation. We are changed by what we eat as well as by what is eating us, what we control and what has us under control, what we plan and work for, and what takes us by surprise going bump in the night. So we have heard not only this week, but countless times in our musings about conversion. And as all that is true about an individual, so it is with communities and human institutions. In that regard, the Church is not significantly different.

Over twenty years ago, in prayerful assembly, some two thousand special custodians of the people's spiritual inheritance examined the condition of the branches on the vine. Some pruning and redirecting, even some uprooting and transplanting were proposed for the life and worship of a worldwide community. Ways of proceeding to meet the changing demands of the twentieth century were adopted in sixteen separate documents. Perhaps the initiators of this Church renewal anticipated a smooth process through the reworking of texts and ritual actions and by tidying up certain ecclesiastical structures. Few, it seems, fully understood that an organic system like people at prayer, when prodded to change, cannot be neatly reshaped like a stone mansion. The stones are living. The change meant conversion by death-resurrection. Some who see it now would like to "go back to Go and collect their two hundred dollars." Still the response to the challenge was beginning to emerge. A conversion of the Church was begun and the rest is a history of fits and starts, forward and backward, some rejoicing, some crying, and a good deal of yawning as well. Surely we've barely begun, and there are signs of a loss of nerve here and there.

A score of years ago the Council Fathers enunciated some very important principles. They were meant to serve as touchstones and power centers for the process of communal change, the conversion of the Church meeting the challenge of a new age. Returning to those principles with fresh attention may serve us well as we try to negotiate successfully our way through to the future. There are two which I would like to isolate and explore with you, because I think they have been implied in our reflections this week, even more so because I think they are so central to the reform. One is from the Constitution on the Church. The other is from the Constitution on the Sacred Liturgy.

In the first two chapters of *Lumen Gentium*, the Church is spoken of most frequently under the metaphor of the people of God "as pilgrims in a strange land" (1:7). In the Constitution on the Sacred Liturgy we read that "in the restoration and promotion of the sacred liturgy . . . full and active participation by all the people is the aim to be considered before all else; for it is the primary and indispensible source from which the faithful derive the true Christian spirit" (1:14). This richly ambiguous metaphor, the pilgrim people of God, and this overarching principle of liturgical reform, *actuosa participatio*, form together, I claim, the centerpiece of imagination about what the Church is trying to do in the whole reform, its institutional conversion. They show the essence of the council. They function as well as principles for evaluation of our ongoing reform. We must retain a strong link to these reference points, if we want to remain true to the challenge. Let's examine each in its turn and trace out the implications insofar as the RCIA has helped us to see them.

Initiation Into the Church as the Pilgrim People of God

A pilgrim people is (to wallow in tautology) a journeying people. The pastoral experience of the RCIA over the past decade, if it has done anything, has enshrined the image of journey. In our discussions this week we have traced out the combinations and permutations of the image. But we have all too painfully come to recognize that for all our protestations about catechumens being initiated into a journeying community, the post-Pentecost experience is more often one of settling into the pew rather than chucking the American Express and setting out on the road. I think that is because on the whole we haven't yet made the full shift from a deductive style of ministry to the world to an inductive one.

Now that merits fuller exposition. Barbara O'Dea, with her careful wisdom, and Regis Duffy, with his eschatological passion, have warned us. Still not trusting our ability to respond with fresh awareness to the new challenges that come our way, we count more on application of behavioral principles rather than to the generation of them in gospel energized pastoral experience. In spite of workshop calls to the contrary, we still favor the classroom over the prayer-room, the logical argument over the surprising insight, the *opus Dei* over the *mirabilia Dei*. It is the difference between the measured conclusions of sacraments' committees and the daring conclusions of the base community that I am trying to ferret out. Our catechumenate communities, dwelling on the liturgy of the Word (breaking open the Word, as the jargon would have it) are in fact doing that. They *are* dwelling in the Word, at least while they are still catechumens. The effect of that dwelling is coming to see the need of, and the way to, fresh world-gospel critical interaction. They may well be the North American counterpart to the *comunidades de base* of Latin America. They probably should be in just as much trouble as their South American counterparts. That may well turn out to be the case if they aren't too quickly assimilated into cultural compromise coupled with the reasonable approach of school modeled theology.

Intense engagement of the Scriptures for the sake of the journey to which one is committed leads to a participant's knowledge of the gospel, not an observer's knowledge. Praxis theology is not the mere accumulation of correct quiz answers; rather it is for the sake of decision and action. It is not school theology. The point is not to claim that school theology is not valuable. In fact it is crucial in its own way. Cut adrift from it our pastoral practice is condemned to repeat the mistakes that plagued our ancestors. But such theology is valuable reflection on a pilgrim's experience. It is not the diet for the pilgrim's journey. It cannot pretend to be that food. Theological conclusions are not the Word of John 6. I think Regis Duffy set us straight on that one. But catechumens aren't the only pilgrims. We all are. Initiation, as Tim Shaughnessy pointed out, doesn't mean membership in a club of those who have arrived, but partnership in a future-oriented enterprise, a kingdom search in common life. None of this is very new information, is it? But unless somehow in midair we abort the leap after Linus' blanket, we have some consequences to suffer. It's time to suffer them.

We have to dare much more than we have in the past or we will find ourselves protecting a cultural curiosity that real journeying people will want to pass by. Perhaps some already have. But my goal here is to engender realistic hope, not merely to grandstand you with jeremiads. (Tim Shaughnessy isn't the only one to shrink from that task. But, then again, it is sometimes hard to tell the difference between the prophet's worldly anguish and the whiney carping of the disappointed idealist). Still it is necessary, I think, to point out that the stakes are very high in this challenge to accept an inductive style of ministry in the world, this dwelling in the Word. I think we have to look at them with courage. For one it means that pluralism is on the increase, not the decline. We have to suffer the consequence. That means unity in the Church is more and more going to be a matter of opposites in dialogue than a leveled out uniformity. The days of claiming there is a universal Catholic behavior are done. Rather than stronger certainty about our claims and clear visions of the future, we will be faced with more penetrating questions about them. Those questions do not arise out of classroom disputes; rather, they are of the more ambiguous kind that surface when people try to live with honesty and integrity in a shrinking and far more complexly interdependent world. For example, Roman Catholics with lifestyles that earlier would have meant their exclusion from the Church have decided not to leave. Furthermore, their reasons for staying are that they intend to represent their minority opinions from the inside. Divorced and remarried, active gays, and a large number of dissatisfied feminists, for example, see a different future, one fashioned out of more discontinuity than an institutional mindset would find comfortable. These people are saying that God is present wherever you let *her* in. Such people aren't taking their marbles and going home, and they will not accept the judgment that they do not belong.

The catechumenate, with the predilection for the inductive style, may well be one forum that nurtures such a pluralism. Are we ready for that? Anyone who dares to try to tame that may find that he/she is tackling a beast far more powerful than disobedient childen. Questioning authority is not about to wane. Some people have discovered that there is power at the base of the pyramid. The challenge for us is not to fear the pluralism but to embrace it, not naively or uncritically, but courageously and hopefully. There is where we may well find the cross in institutional conversion. We have far to go indeed. Emmaus is up ahead.

We're still not at the bottom of our search for implications to a full reading of the metaphor of the pilgrim people of God. All I have examined with you so far points out the crucial need to find spirit-filled ways to deal with the conflicts, uncertainties, and disputes that inevitably will arise. I think it means we are challenged to develop two gifts that belong to the whole community, but which too easily atrophy from disuse, and they are necessary not only for catechumenal ministry. They are contemplation and discernment.

One can hear what one wants when listening to the Gospels. Opposing sides can take up the same holy book and use it to defend their position, even in violent and abusive ways. One solution would be to impose the same moral and juridical interpretation of the gospel, enunciating principles of behavior for all. But that is a return to a deductive method. It would be a kind of foreclosure wherein the interpretation co-opts the fresh gospel experience. It will not work, especially in this third age of the world Church. Rather, it is necessary to teach discernment, to adopt ways to know whether true charity, faithful consistency, living coherency and right continuity are being served when one claims to see with the gospel light. We have far to go to help one another discover whether we are putting bags over our heads or taking them off. We have far to go in learning how to let the gospel convert us rather than subtly using the gospel to fortify our unquestioned assumptions and prejudices. That goes for the theologians and liturgy commissions and Church officials as well as for the Chilean peasants. The secret for dealing with divergence and disagreement in the catechumenate and elsewhere is not to stop the inductive process of discovery and desire, or to disarm it, but to deepen it, extend it, and channel it.

Contemplation involves an act of surrender to the Word, an attitude of courageous reverence for the truth and an expectation that God's fidelity will show up in this one consistency: he always surprises us. Discernment is a tool to help gauge the truth of that surrender, the adequacy of that reverence, and the honesty of that expectation of surprise. They are acts, attitudes, and tools only for pilgrims headed for the Kingdom. Contemplation and discernment presuppose a future of open possibilities. They will be unintelligible for those who favor conclusions over search, satiation over thirst, or comfort over yearning. One is never done with change. Death-resurrection is a way of life, not only a one time event. To embrace the death of what is for the sake of the new life yet to be seen is to allow the Word of God to be not only a word of information, but also, and more powerfully, a Word of promise cherished in the heart. And promise only has meaning for those who cannot rely on their own reserves, their own vision, bank accounts, credentials, titles, even on nuclear warheads (of either the military or ecclesiastical kind).

Before moving on to our closer look at the principle of active participation, I want to hazard one other specifically outrageous claim about the effect of all this pluralism on sacramental praxis theology. It is a corollary to the ecclesial questions we have examined so far under the heading of the metaphor of the pilgrim People of God. I speak what follows not out of tested conclusions and experience, but out of suspicion. Consider it a bit of fishing in the dark, if you will. But test it yourselves in some secret place in your cerebellum, where you give safe harbor to your favorite heresies.

We've seen worm can lids strewn about the floor of this meeting. They were opened up in our frustration over how to deal with the various position statements on the RCIA. I suggest that somewhere in our collective psyche we know we are running a little scared. We are quite dissatisfied with the initiation sacramental discipline we have inherited. RCIA, with its roots in a "patristic" sacramentality, has not well cohabited with the other sacramental disciplines of initiation handed on to us before. Still we are not sure whether we are in over our heads trying to deal with all that. There are hints that our neat scholastic sacramental theological system is in serious trouble. We learned at our mother's knee that all the sacraments were carefully tagged and numbered, as if the tag gave more than a name, and as if the number seven were a sacrosanct number. A closer reading of Trent may well show that it is not so sacrosanct as we thought. And walls were set up around those sacraments clearly marking their separation, one from the other. "Here is the matter and form of baptism, here and nowhere else." Apologetic sacramental theology uttered for one reason has been expected to serve as a pastoral one as well. But pastoral practice is showing us something different which we may not be eager to admit aloud. It is time to come out of the closet (to mix the metaphor) and admit that the tag names are fading and the dividing walls are showing some cracks. In the catechumenal experience, this taste of patristic rather than scholastic sacramentality, sacramental liturgy is showing up less as an extrinsic event and more as a series of privileged moments in a symbiotic relationship with process. That's heady stuff.

There are some unsettled theological matters tucked inside our pastoral practice. I'd like to tease out a few of them. Is the catechumenal process, and especially the transitional rites, a preparation for or a participation in the sacrament? What will it mean for the integrity of the sacraments when "three," baptism, confirmation, and Eucharist, are celebrated consistently in one single prayer event? What does it mean when bishops are celebrating fewer confirmations and more elections? What does it mean when private, auricular confession is celebrated in Lent for those who come to our table for the first time in full communion as baptized but uncatechized Protestants?

The last word is far from in on all of these in regard to baptism. What will happen when we finally begin the reform of penance in a process mode? Where will it all end? I think we had good reasons to be skittish about the position statements. We may not yet be ready to go fishing with all these worms. Certainly no one is ready to have to eat them.

Initiation into a Participatory Church

Just as the full appropriation of the Church's self descriptive metaphor of the pilgrim People of God ought to issue forth in a shift of pastoral theological method, so the principle of active participation signals a powerful shift of gravity in the Church's self understanding about being a people at prayer. My claim is that we have barely begun to see what that means. But let me not race ahead. Let's take some careful steps.

Certainly one measure of the quality of the liturgical reform, one important piece of institutional conversion, is the level of reading one allows to the principle of active participation. It can mean many things depending on whether one gives it a strong or weak interpretation. The weakest might sound like this: "Active participation means that the lay folk can do something to help Father with his Mass." Another nearly as anemic a reading would sound like this: "Get the people to sing more; start a folk group, or a dance group." All that is good enough as far as it goes. But like T. S. Eliot's description of the Fourth Temptor, that may well be the matter of the highest reason, doing the right thing for the wrong reason. Active participation is a matter of the right reason—better to say the right imagination—than of right activity alone. Put another way, participation is not an extrinsic principle; it is an intrinsic one. That means, for example, that worship is not something which happens whether or not the people are there. Worship is the people at prayer. Sacraments are not performed by powerful ordained others over against, on top of, or on behalf of people without that power. Sacrament occurs in the midst of the properly assembled community already constituted in power. The RCIA puts it this way: "The initiation of adults is the business of all the baptized." I think we have yet to take that to heart in our practice. We have yet to see what it will be like when everyone takes an interest in the family business.

Active participation is first of all a claim about the spirit which animates a community, a spirit given in power to a people as a people, immersed in the death-resurrection of Christ. The Greeks had a word for that immersion; it is *baptizein*. That essential power, that animation for worship in spirit and truth which belongs to the whole body united to its head, was recognized by no less a luminary than Thomas Aquinas who acknowledged that baptism deputizes one for worship. Aidan Kavanagh, never at a loss for an aphorism, has claimed that one is baptized a priest and ordained a presbyter. We have far to go to find out what all that could mean. Maybe when we get to Emmaus we'll know.

Consider this, too, from the unique pastoral perspective of our day as the RCIA gradually gains attention. For the first time in about fourteen hundred years, the Church once again has a visible order of catechumens seeking to become members of the order of the faithful. One effect of that is that the order of faithful is given a new meaning by the catechumens' petition for admittance. No longer need the term "faithful" appear in popular reading of juridic pronouncements as what is left over after the real Church, the clergy, has been served. All this leads to the simple yet powerfully liberating recognition that in the catechumenate the Church is making a shift from an ordination-weighted model of life and worship to a baptismal one. But we have far to go. Baptismal spirituality is not very deep seated in our experience. We have to pursue the meaning of being a member of the order of the faithful. For presbyters, for example, that means a little less attention to what priests can do, and should be doing, and more attention to the overlooked fact that before a priest is leader of the assembly he is a member of the assembly. The second indelible mark didn't erase the first one. Ironically, that is a taproot of the problem of clericalism. I don't want to level another salvo against the ordained. In fact, as a priest myself, I am tiring of being the easiest target no matter how deserving of the opprobrium. But truth to tell, I'm not sure that staff professionalism is an advance over clericalism, and of this I am sure: parish council bickering is definitely *not* an advance at all. The problem of clericalism is perhaps less one of a leadership question and more a membership one. We priests aren't too sure about how to be members of the faithful. And I doubt that is only our fault. I think in part it is a manifestation of the systematic evil of a deductive style. You can call that style "seminary" if you like. You'll be close to the mark. Furthermore, no priest who has participated in the inductive process of nurturing another's conversion to full life as a member of the faithful has left that experience without being changed himself, and changed first of all precisely as a believer. That's quite exciting and quite unsettling. Perhaps we're seeing the beginning of an overdue priests' lib. Hang on, bigger things are coming. We're not at Emmaus yet.

But I think there is something even more basic to consider than all I have addressed so far under this heading of *actuosa participatio*. I think the catechumenal journey of conversion is challenging the whole praying Church to take a look at the most basic issue in the ecclesial life of prayer. We are shaken to the root. It has to do with our assumptions about what it means to be a people at prayer at all. Liturgy is not first of all an occasion for prayer. Liturgy is prayer itself. It is a corporate prayer in which the "we" precedes the "I." I think that is the principle Barbara O'Dea was eloquently addressing. Liturgy is corporate prayer. What happens when that fully shows up in our deepest level of assumptions about ourselves? What kind of revolutionary alteration of human consciousness would that signal? It is the body which glorifies God, as Regis Duffy reminded us. But does the body believe it is one body and one body only? I don't want merely to point out our need to build vibrant communities. I'm after something more basic, namely the need to recognize how deep is our human solidarity at birth even before we decide to do anything about it. Let me go about this in a *via negativa*.

Avery Dulles once claimed that the doctrine of original sin is "closed for repairs." I'm about ready to claim that it has returned from the shop with added horsepower. The name for original sin may well be believing in the lie of our alienation. Another name for it is individualism. In our Western culture our taken-for-granted imagination is backwards. There is a disorder at the very origins of our imagination. Our problem is not first of all making community happen, but discovering that human community is inescapable. Our fundamental sin has to do with our futile and tragic attempts to escape our deep unity in our common poverty, running from it, clubbing each other to get ahead rather than to remain in solidarity, and "Tylenoling" ourselves into a nirvana world of avoidance of the pain of living for real. The world is full of pain relievers for everywhere it hurts, Anacin, Pepto-Bismol, and Preparation H.

The truth is that we start out as one, deeply one in root. Your joys are mine, your pains are mine; I am diminished by your diminishment, and exalted along with you. The rudimentary puzzle is not how to bridge the gap between people, but rather how we ever came to believe that the apparent gap between us was real to start with. Who fed us this apple?

The frustration of St. Paul with the Corinthians was about this very matter. They were living fractured lives when in truth they were one. They were sacramentalizing a lie by eating in separation. They gave in to individualism and the myth of privilege. Theirs wasn't the awareness of a Teilhard who saw that each person was the whole universe from one perspective, or of a John Donne who said in his day before inclusive language that no "man" is an island. Our challenge at its deepest is not to be fooled into thinking that my physical body circumscribes a radically independent individual, that this parish exists as radically independent from the larger Church, or that the Church is meant to do other than be a significant, transformative part of the larger world. The liturgy leaps beyond those appearances and raises up the truth of the one bread and the one body. Active participation means recognizing the one bread and the one body by worshipping as an assembly finding as much real presence in one another as in the Word and the bread and the cup. And above all, active participation means recognizing in the broken bread the surprising crucified one. The one we thought was dead is alive in our assembly. He is the one who makes it possible for us to be active participants in a pilgrim way of common life.

We do have a long way to go, but we go with a lot of hope. Not because we see what is ahead, but because we pilgrims share food for our journey. And while our hearts may still be burning within us, we can be sure once again that certain strangers among us, the poor, the left-overs, catechumens, and other such little ones will show us where we are really going when we let them sit down and eat with us. They will let us know that while we thought we were only heading for the little village of our figured-out Emmaus, we are really heading for a whole new surprising Kingdom. We have far to go, so for God's sake and our own let's not stop now.

AUTHORS

REGIS A. DUFFY, O.F.M., is currently a professor at The Washington Theological Union and has been visiting professor at Princeton Theological Seminary and at the University of Notre Dame. Father Regis holds seven academic degrees among which are two degrees from the *Institut de Liturgie* of Paris and a doctorate in sacramental theology from the *Institut Catholique* of Paris. He has also done post-doctoral work in Paris at *Hautes Etudes*, Sorbonne University. On a recent sabbatical he did research at the University of Wurzburg, W. Germany. Father Regis is involved in reeducation and pastoral workshops here and abroad. He has been sacramental-area editor for the *Supplement of The New Catholic Encyclopedia* and has published articles in *Worship, Theologie der Gegenwart, The Heythrop Journal, The Proceedings of the Catholic Theological Society of America, The Journal of Ecumenical Studies,* and in recent collections such as *The Sacraments: God's Love and Mercy Actualized* and *Liturgy and Social Justice.* Father Regis' book *Real Presence* was published in 1982. Since then he has authored *A Roman Catholic Theology of Pastoral Care* and *On Becoming a Catholic: The Challenge of Initiation.*

JAMES D. SHAUGHNESSY is currently pastor of St. Cecilia Parish in Peoria, Illinois, a position he undertook after completing his work as the first director of the Murphy Center for Liturgical Research at the University of Notre Dame. He holds a master's degree in economics from The Catholic University of America and a master's degree in liturgical research from the University of Notre Dame. A member of the original board and first chairman of the Federation of Diocesan Liturgical Commissions, Father Shaughnessy has served as an advisor to the Bishops' Committee on the Liturgy, a member of the International Committee for English in the Liturgy, a member of the Board of Directors of the North American Liturgical Conference, and a charter member of the North American Academy of Liturgy. Father Shaughnessy has been involved in all phases of pastoral work, including membership on the Illinois Division of the U.S. Commission for Civil Rights and the Roman Catholic/United

Methodist Consultation. In 1976, Father Shaughnessy was the recipient of the Michael Mathis Award from the University of Notre Dame.

BARBARA O'DEA, D.W., is director of liturgy in the Diocese of Pueblo, Colorado. After special studies at The Catholic University of America, Murphy Center for Liturgical Research, and Iona College, she received her M.A. from the Graduate Theological Union, Berkeley, in 1979. In her present position, Sister Barbara directs liturgical ministry formation programs and serves as a resource person to parish catechumenates throughout the Diocese of Pueblo. In addition she is a lecturer on liturgy and ecclesiology in the diocesan diaconate program. The author of *Of Fast and Festival* and *The Once and Future Church (RCIA)*, Sister Barbara has published extensively on initiation and conversion in *Modern Liturgy, Chicago Catechumenate, New Catholic World*, and *Celebration*. She is a contributing editor of *Service*, resources for pastoral ministry.

JAMES LOPRESTI, S.J., is director of the Loyola Pastoral Institute in New York. Presently a member of the faculty of the Seminary of the Immaculate Conception in Huntington, New York, he also has taught liturgical theology at Loyola University of Chicago and Weston School of Theology. He has pastoral experience of the RCIA from as early as 1974, serving as a member of, or consultant to, parish catechumenate teams in Boston, Chicago, and New York. He completed his Ph.D. at Boston University in 1981, writing his dissertation on conversion in the RCIA. Father Lopresti has given numerous workshops on the catechumenate in the United States and Canada. His articles on liturgy have appeared in *Worship, New Catholic World, Hosanna*, and *Christian Initiation Resources*. A founding member of the North American Academy of Liturgy, he is also a member of the steering committee of the North American Forum on the Catechumenate.

Read Article by Rambo p. 32 - 1+2
Robb p. 54